100 WEIRD WAYS
TO CATCH FISH

100 WEIRD WAYS TO CATCH FISH

John Waldman

STACKPOLE
BOOKS

Published by
STACKPOLE BOOKS
5067 Ritter Road
Mechanicsburg, PA 17055
www.stackpolebooks.com

Printed in the United States

First edition

10 9 8 7 6 5 4 3 2 1

Cover design by Wendy A. Reynolds
Art credits on page 191

Library of Congress Cataloging-in-Publication Data

Waldman, John R.
    100 weird ways to catch fish / John Waldman.—1st ed.
      p. cm.
    ISBN 0-8117-3179-0 (alk. paper)
    1. Fishing—Miscellanea. I. Title: One hundred weird ways to catch fish.
II. Title.

SH441.W33 2005
799.1—dc22   2004027369

To BeBe and Richie, my original fishing partners.

Yet fish there be, that
neither hook nor line

Nor snare, nor net, nor
engine can make thine.

John Bunyan

Pilgrim's Progress (1678)

ACKNOWLEDGMENTS

The idea for this book arose from a conversation with Rob Maass. From there, I plumbed the very best fishing minds I could find among friends, acquaintances, and a few very helpful strangers, including Robert Boyle, Chris D'Elia, Malcolm Gilbert, Joseph Hightower, Walter Hingley, Warwick Kershaw, Tom Lake, Rob Maass, Tommy McPartland, John McPhee, Fen Montaigne, Mike Oliver, Steve Quinn, Dave Rosane, Steve Sautner, Misha Skopets, Dave Taft, Ed Van Put, Beth Waterman, David West, and David Yozzo. Judith Schnell and Amy Lerner of Stackpole Books provided enthusiastic support along the way.

I also thank my home team, Carol, Laura, and Stevie, for family time foregone as I cast about through fishing history.

INTRODUCTION

Fish live in water.

This incontrovertible fact is extremely inconvenient for those who seek them. Nonetheless, human beings have endeavored to extract fish from their native habitat for eons before recorded history. Fishing scenes can be viewed on cave walls, fish remains are prominent in archaeological digs, and low river waters sometimes reveal ancient fishing weirs. Yet despite our vast experience, we still struggle to land fish, and often they win. Fish may be tantalizingly visible while we peer from a bridge or riverbank, or while they leap a waterfall, or while we swim or dive, or even as we monitor them electronically with sophisticated fish-finders, but detecting their presence is not the same as actually placing them in the bucket, creel, or the hold of a ship. Fish (with the possible exception of wild brown trout on hard-fished streams) are not geniuses, but they occur in a distinctly foreign and difficult habitat for humans and are endowed with natural survival instincts, both of which make their capture no small challenge.

Despite these obstacles, the superb food and sport that fish provide have caused the catching of fish to be one of mankind's longest running obsessions. It started simply. In *Fishing from the Earliest Times* (1921), William Radcliffe reconstructed the origins of fishing as likely having occurred in four stages. First came fishing with the hand, which he surmised took place for fish left half-stranded in small pools by tides or floods or for fish spawning in the shallows. Second came spear hunting, used originally on fish lying in pools deep enough to prevent hand fishing. Third came fishing with a line, perhaps invented by someone who witnessed how dropped morsels of food in a pool were seized by fish. The problem of how to reach and land them was solved by the method—christened by Sheringham as "entanglement by appetite"—achieved by fastening a gorge through a thorn holding some kind of bait to an animal sinew. Last came fishing with a net. Radcliffe's theory is that a primitive piscator, when trying to catch fish by hand in small pools, blocked any little exits with plaited twigs, which was the precursor of the woven net.

Whether or not Radcliffe got the details right, there is a certain fundamental logic to these approaches—they encompass most of the rational possibilities for catching fish. In fact, he observed that fishing techniques have changed less over the centuries than have corresponding techniques in, say, hunting (changed by the introduction of the gun), and that the spear, the line and hook, and the net have remained preeminent. But even within this realm there have been numerous clever variations—and then there are the really odd methods that stray far beyond them.

My book is a survey of the many ingenious means people have invented to catch fish through history and around the world, celebrating what I believe are the stranger methods at the expense of the more mundane. Some approaches may not appear unusual to the reader if they already are familiar with them; that is, ayu fishing and haul seining, which are not novelties to their practitioners, but either might seem fantastic to the other. My survey cannot possibly be complete, but the techniques presented are a healthy sampling that bear witness to the compelling allure of these finned creatures and to the remarkable lengths to which fishermen extend themselves to outwit them. On that last point, I do not condone the illegal methods described. Although some practical knowledge is imparted, this is not a how-to manual; it's an appreciation of the sheer imagination and resourcefulness applied to the problem of catching fish.

I also make little distinction among recreational, subsistence, and commercial fishing. Some recreational anglers have long sold all or part of their catches and many also fish for their own protein. Also, both subsistence and commercial fishermen often take great pleasure in working their gear and nets. Landing giant tuna in the *mattanza* of Sicily, for example, is so compelling that it never could become dull.

And sometimes the boundaries between recreational and commercial fishing are strangely blurred. J. H. Hall in *Selling Fish* (2000) described recreational gill netting, the perverse practice of cordoning off a cove with the net and thrashing the water to drive the fish toward it. Hall found it beguiling to watch the cork floats dance, sink, and resurface as the fish entered the meshes. Admitting it is a highly unusual practice, he then would let his catch go. Earlier, Thoreau touched on this blending of motivations when he described an old man who lived along the Concord River, writing that "His fishing was not a sport, nor solely a means of subsistence, but a sort of solemn sacrament and withdrawal from the world. . . ."

Necessity, and its partner, desire, have mothered remarkable invention. So universal has been this quest for fish that I invite you as you journey through my one hundred ways to think of a reasonable, or even offbeat, approach that has not been tried. The challenge remains. After all, fish live in water, and we don't.

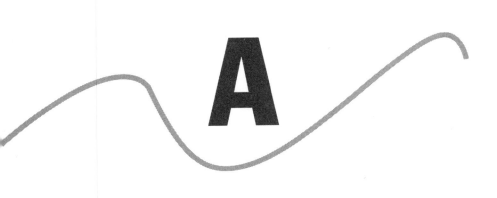

A

AERIAL FISHING

A fish already out of water is half the battle won

Many fish leap to escape from danger below, and fishermen have developed all kinds of clever gear to take advantage of this. After all, if the fisherman's goal is to remove fish from the water, seeking leaping fish gives him a great head start.

The species most apt to leap (other than salmon at waterfalls) is mullet, a rather cosmopolitan fish. Around the world, fishermen have invented ingenious ways to pluck jumping mullet. The simplest of tricks often was used in Lake Vrana, Yugoslavia. A small boat was fixed slightly obliquely across the lake's outlet. Mullet ascending from the sea would encounter this barrier, attempt to vault it, and in the process, land in the boat, ready for delivery.

Catching gray mullet with a boat in the outlet of Lake Vrana, Yugoslavia.

Over much of the Mediterranean, Black, and Caspian Seas, jumping mullet were caught using rafts of reeds. On a moonlit night, mullet saw the shadow cast by a raft floating on the water surface and appeared to perceive it as an obstacle, so they would

1

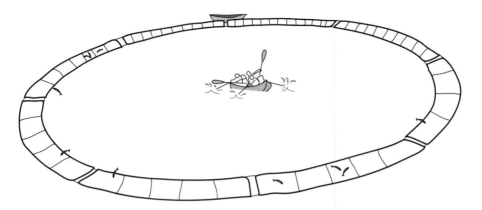

Floating rafts used by Russians for catching mullet in the Caspian Sea.

try to leap over it. But the rafts made to catch fish were wide enough (four to twelve feet) that the airborne mullet would not clear them and wound up flopping on top. To prevent them from wriggling back into the water, the edges of the rafts were bent upward. Sometimes brushwood and netting also were used to entangle the fish.

In England, a ruse was used to keep mullet that had been corralled from leaping out of the net. By breaking up a bale of hay so that the floating "headline" of the net was buffered by a couple feet of floating straw, any mullet leaping would take off too soon, thereby landing within the net's confines.

The Chinese designed an especially sophisticated method of catching leaping fish. They suspended a net wall from stakes below and above the water. On both sides of the emergent portion of the net hung net bags conveniently poised to catch fish that bounced off the net wall. Perhaps there is good reason that we define helplessness as "a fish out of water."

ARTIFICIAL REEFS

The strange allure of junk in the water

Reef is a catchall term for many kinds of structures, natural or otherwise, that extend above the seafloor. Fish are innately attracted to such structures as places to hide or to find food, and they undoubtedly aggregate at reefs. Sponges, corals, barnacles, clams, and other encrusting organisms colonize both natural and artificial reefs, and as food sources, they may even increase fish production. Some regions along the Atlantic coast, such as New England, have abundant bedrock and boulder reefs, so there is not much need for artificial reefs. But south of Long Island, New York, the coastal plain is almost featureless, and consequently, interest in artificial reefs is much higher.

In 2003, fifty thirty-year-old brick-colored New York City subway cars called Redbirds were dropped into the ocean off New Jersey with fanfare. Opinions about this were polarized: Advocates believed that marine creatures fancy artificial reefs, whereas detractors said that it was an excuse to dump trash in the ocean. Divers immediately followed the cars down to record their undersea reception and found curious fish already passing through their doors.

Ships that sink because of war, weather, or accidents frequently form excellent artificial reefs for fishing. Also, derelict ships often are purposely sunk worldwide for use as artificial reefs. Florida alone has more than one hundred of them. A diver-based survey demonstrated their attractiveness to sea creatures compared with nearby natural reefs. Although the natural reefs had a greater number of total species, the reefs created from the ships had greater fish abundance and species diversity.

Today artificial reefs usually fall into one of two classes. Some are constructed from building materials, such as log cribs sunk together with concrete blocks, stacked fiberglass cylinders, or concrete geodesic or modular structures that resemble oversize children's assembly toys. Research has shown that the state-of-the-art reef-building material is the reef ball, essentially an igloo-shaped sphere with large holes to allow fish to swim in and out. The three-foot-high and four-foot-diameter spheres are poured from concrete and weigh a hefty fourteen hundred pounds. Some are made by inmates at correctional facilities. So effective are reef balls that there now is a Reef Ball Foundation, which had conducted projects in forty-eight nations as of this writing.

Other artificial reefs are made from materials recycled from other societal applications—what are called "materials of convenience." This category is larger and perhaps more interesting. Sunken military aircraft, automobiles, steel and concrete bridges, concrete culvert pipes, steel and dry dock work platforms, oil refinery hardware, refrigerators, toilets, and even intercontinental ballistic missiles draw fish in large numbers. Many army tanks have been deposited in New Jersey waters, because the state's Fort Dix Army Base is federally certified for stripping and sanitizing armored vehicles prior to being jettisoned. Old tires and other smaller objects have been used, but they tend to drift away with storm currents. But if tires are wired together as pyramids and weighted with concrete, they become much more stationary and attractive to fish.

Oil drilling platforms have become a primary angling resource on the flat bottom of the Gulf of Mexico, these seafloor-to-surface structures attracting different species to all watery layers, from red snapper on the bottom to king mackerel on top. Some of these platforms have fallen out of use, and in an innovative program to aid anglers, the oil industry has made an agreement with the state of Texas to leave the rigs behind to serve as reefs and to provide the money saved from not having to remove them to the state to help fund its artificial reef program.

ASCENDING LURES FOR ATTRACTING LINGCOD

A clever tease

Native Americans on the Pacific Northwest coast knew that always-voracious lingcod are attracted to anything that moves like a smaller fish. They learned to pull lingcod toward the surface with a clever visual attraction system, then spear or dip-net them from canoes in these clear Pacific waters. The fisherman used a long pole to push a hand-carved wooden lure down into the water. After the pole was disengaged, the lure fluttered and revolved slowly back toward the surface, drawing hungry lingcod behind it along the way. The lures were a fine blend of utilitarian function and folk art, often having splayed wings resembling a badminton shuttlecock to provide swimming action, but with heads chiseled to resemble a wolf or fish.

Real fish also could be used as attractors. The fisherman filled the stomach of a greenling or tomcod with pebbles for weight, sometimes slicing off one fillet to make it move erratically. This hookless bait could be dangled from a rope to entice lingcod within harvesting range.

ASPHYXIATION FISHING

Unexciting, but breathless nonetheless

The monkey fish of Australia live in holes in the coral reefs. One way of procuring these otherwise difficult-to-catch fish is to force them to use up their oxygen. The method is straightforward, though less than sporting. At low tide, a thick layer of a native grass is placed over the fish's hole and then secured with a large rock. Upon returning at the next low tide twelve hours later, the fisherman should find the monkey fish floating at the top of its burrow, asphyxiated.

AUTOMATIC JIGGING MACHINES

They don't need coffee breaks

Commercial fishing is, well, commercial, and commercial fishermen constantly seek any advantages that will provide more fish per hour or dollar expended. One way for commercial hook and line fishermen to add "labor" without adding salaries is to "hire" automatic jigging machines. Fish caught individually this way also may be worth more on the market, as they are not dragged around and damaged as in some net fisheries. Automatic jigging machines also are environmentally friendly, because little bycatch is killed, as occurs in so many other commercial fisheries, where the wrong fish also are caught and injured in the process.

These electrically or hydraulically powered machines have strong line wound on large-spool reels, which are mounted on short, stout rods. Unlike traditional handlines, best fished one line per fisherman, an operator can work three jigging machines at once. In Iceland, forty-foot double-ended Norwegian high-sided trawlers have been outfitted with automatic jigging machines spaced three feet apart. When a jigging machine's line hits bottom, it goes slack and then is lifted about two feet. When it loads up with hooked fish that exceed a certain threshold of tension, the machine automatically hauls them up.

In a test comparison in Alaska between a single automatic jigging machine and a standard halibut longline, the jigging machine generated more raw poundage of fish, although the longline produced more marketable poundage. The jigging machine caught lingcod, pollock, Pacific cod, and four kinds of rockfish. When it fished six lures simultaneously, it harvested fish at the impressive rate of eleven hundred pounds per hour, even though about half the time was lost in repositioning the boat over productive bottom.

AYU FISHING

Turf battles can be deadly

When an angler casts bait, it normally is to entice a fish into striking it as food. Not so when ayu fishing. Here the lure resembles another ayu, and the live fish only wants to drive the intruder away.

Ayu is a smeltlike relative of trout found in streams across the Japan archipelago, where they are considered a symbol of the countryside and being at one with nature. The young migrate to sea and return in March to ascend coastal rivers. They are short-lived, surviving for only about twelve months, and thus are known as *nen-gyo*, or "year-fish." It is said that the Japanese people feel sorry for them because of their brief existence. Revered for their aromatic flavor, they also are called "sweetfish" and the "queen of freshwater streams."

Ayu are difficult to catch by the usual angling methods, because they feed by scraping algae off rocks with their saw-shaped teeth. But the ayu has a behavioral trait that renders it vulnerable to anglers: It claims its own "turf," attacking and driving away any other ayu that tries to invade it. A single ayu's territory measures about one hundred to two hundred square feet.

Near Kyoto some three hundred years ago, anglers learned to take advantage of this territorial behavior with a live-lure technique called *tomo-zuri*. In this method, the fisherman ties a live ayu to a line by its gills, fits it with three or four special hooks along its underside, and then guides this "baitfish" with a very long rod (as long as thirty to thirty-three feet) into the lair of another. The owner of the territory will keep its eyes on the interloper and, when it becomes apparent that the intruder is not leaving, will attack it by ramming its belly, thereby getting hooked, usually a little behind the head.

When the tethered baitfish eventually becomes exhausted, the angler replaces it with a freshly caught ayu. Fine lines are used to avoid tiring an ayu quickly; modern technology has produced metal threads for this purpose as thin as forty microns in diameter. Because of their great length, lightweight rods are most appreciated; the very lightest can cost as much as $5,000.

In earlier centuries, ayu were accepted in Japan as payment for taxes. Today ayu is associated with summer in that nation in the same way that grilled hot dogs and hamburgers are in the United States. The fish is impaled headfirst on a stick, salted, and cooked over hot coals. Unfortunately, dams have diminished ayu runs. But public realization of the decline in population of this cultural icon has led to greater environmental awareness in Japan.

BAMBOO BRIDGE FISHING

An engineer's delight

Fishing from temporary bamboo bridges is a rather contemplative Asian method that requires much preparation. The bamboo bridge is really a personal platform over a carefully chosen location on a lake or river. The fisherman lashes green bamboo sticks together across two supporting rocks about two feet above the water level. To catch fish, he uses a lift net made from plant fiber. The net measures about four feet square, and its four corners are tied to thin bamboo poles held in the fisherman's hands. Before fishing, he places white stone slabs on the bottom both to attract fish and to provide a bright background against which to observe them.

When all is set, the fisherman crouches and watches. If he is fortunate, a school of snow trout will move in, at which time he brings the bamboo poles together and snatches the rig smartly upward. Bamboo bridge fishing works best during dry season; monsoons roil the water too much. When conditions are right, a skilled practitioner may land twenty pounds of fish per day.

BANK POLING AND LIMB LINING

Gauntlet in the mud

Bank poles are used in slow southern U.S. rivers to catch catfish. Along with several other passive catfishing techniques, such as trotlining and jugging, bank poling is simple but effective. Cane is the material of choice for bank poles. Guided by the principle that short sticks snap more easily than long, springy ones, fishermen set long poles over likely catfish lairs at an angle of forty-five degrees or less from shore, securing them in the mud. Angle one too high, and it may break under the strain of a hooked fish; angle it too low, and a hooked fish may pull it into the river.

The fisherman ties strong braided fishing line near the base of each pole and then knots it at two-foot intervals all the way to the top; this helps distribute tension while fighting a fish in the same way that round guides do on a modern fishing rod. The amount of line left dangling is about equal to the length of the pole. The fisherman sets up a gauntlet of these outfits, baits the hooks, sits back, and waits for the poles to start bobbing.

A related technique is limb lining. Here the angler ties lines to limber but strong tree branches growing above a river, preferably near an undercut bank. This is said to work well for wary flathead catfish.

BASS STANDS

Gentlemen's pleasure

During the mid-1800s, surf casting for striped bass at selected New York and New England locations using pieces of menhaden for bait was considered, together with Atlantic salmon fishing, to be the pinnacle of game-fishing experiences. In fact, in *Fishing in American Waters* (1869), Genio Scott writes that "casting menhaden bait for striped bass from the rocky shores of the bays, estuaries, and islands along the Atlantic coast constitutes the highest branch of American angling." To facilitate this approach in the rugged environment of breakers and boulders, gentlemen anglers built metal bass stands from which to cast at prime locations, including

Montauk, New York; along the Connecticut and Rhode Island coasts; and on Block Island, Martha's Vineyard, and Nantucket.

The highest refinement of this form of fishing may have been at the private striped-bass fishing clubs located near Buzzard's Bay, Massachusetts. The West Island Club was founded about 1862, and the Cuttyhunk Club in 1865. The clubs were exclusive, made up mainly of wealthy businessmen and politicians from the big cities. Each had the requisite clubhouse and the trappings of the leisure class.

But an essential element was the bass stand, a rickety affair mounted in the most severe of environments. To make a bass stand, the club selected a fishy spot, then drilled a string of boulders or bedrock humps trailing off to the breakers, fitted iron pipes into them as the foundation for a catwalk, built a wooden walk atop the frame, and sometimes placed a chair at the end of the stand.

The "sports"—that is, the gentlemen members—would draw for the best stands the night before fishing. Then, near dawn, they would cast from the stand and wait while a chummer employed by the club fed cut menhaden, clams, crabs, and even lobsters into the surf. If a sport hooked a fish, the chummer did the gaffing.

The bass stands allowed large catches of striped bass in challenging conditions, despite the crude tackle of the time. For instance, in three months' fishing off a stand at Newport, two men landed 124 striped bass weighing 2,921 pounds, an average of more than 23 pounds each, the largest weighing 60 pounds.

In the late 1800s, striped bass went into a coastwide decline, the bass clubs were disbanded, and the platforms began to rust and fall apart from the force of the sea. But even today sharp-eyed surf casters with a historical bent can see remnants of these structures at the still superb striper-fishing locations.

BEE ATTRACTORS

Angry insect equals hungry fish

The bee attractor technique is one that probably is used more in literature than in practice, but a friend read about this and actually tried it. The angler catches a honeybee or bumblebee, puts it in a covered glass jar, makes it angry by shaking it, and then places the bottle in the water tied to a pier. The flittering and buzzing insect drives sunfish and other species crazy, leaving them readily catchable. An alternative is to place minnows in a bottle to attract carnivorous fish such as bass. If you use the bee approach, it's probably best to avoid the insect when you are finished with it.

BOWFISHING

When aiming low pays off

The Bowfishing Association of America has about 500 members, whereas Trout Unlimited has about 125,000 more, but the two groups probably are equally passionate about their sports. With their radically different sensibilities, however, I doubt they'd get along at the dinner table.

Bowfishing is a blood sport, and shoot-and-release is not an option, at least not legally or morally. The bowfisher uses a long bow, either recurved or compound, together with arrows fitted with fish points bearing reversible barbs, a reel and line to retrieve the arrow and fish, and polarized sunglasses. Because light bends, or refracts, when it passes through water, a submerged fish appears closer to the surface than it actually is. Beginning bowfishers are told to aim low, then aim lower, to compensate for this effect.

Bowfishing is not easy; even the most skilled aboriginal Nepalese bowfishers are said to strike only about three of ten targets. Bowfishing also is known from Oceania, south India, Sri Lanka, Burma, Indonesia, Taiwan, and aboriginally throughout much of North and South America. Crossbows were used in the Philippines and south India, the latter a sixteenth-century import from Portugal.

In fresh waters, where most contemporary North American bowfishing is done, common carp are the most frequent target, but many other species are taken. Suckers on their early-spring runs make attractive victims, as do northern pike basking in post–ice-out shallows. Other rough fish that often are legally shot include gar, bowfin, buffalo fish, paddlefish, carpsucker, grass carp, tilapia, and catfish. They are hunted both during the day and at night with lights. A few marine species also are sought with bow and arrow. One is the stingray, which may be visible on sand or mudflats on calm, sunny days. But stingrays are so strong that the hunter risks having the bow yanked out of his hand. A solution is to rig the line to an empty soda bottle and let the fish pull it around and tire itself out for a while before hauling it in.

Bowfishing can lead to some interesting social conflicts. California has ninety-two public piers along its coast, but only the one at Imperial Beach allows hunting fish with bow and arrow. Day and night, bow fishers take stations along the fifteen-hundred-foot-long structure, staring down with arrows drawn for signs of corvina, or white sea bass, their most prized prey. But occasionally the currents bring ocean swimmers, surfers, and boogie boarders within the bowfisher's range, making those at sea level distinctly nervous— and sometimes leading to angry confrontations. The bowfishers are supposed to shoot within twenty feet of the pier, but it's difficult to resist targets within the arrow's range of about thirty yards. People in the water have looked up to find bows pointed right at them. One was quoted as saying, "People in this town are terrified of these guys. Would you let a guy with a gun hunt on a Little League field? Someone's going to get shot." But the president of the Bowfishing Association said that although some accidents within the sport have occurred, most have involved bowfishers shooting other bowfishers.

John McPhee in *The Founding Fish* (2002) describes the unusual bow-and-arrow fishery in the Delaware River for postspawning American shad. Instead of seeking targets from boats or the shore, bowhunters in the upper river build stands on scaffolding that rise three feet from the water surface. From these platforms, they place arrows through the broad, silver targets that are adult shad on their way back to the ocean. Unfortunately, McPhee noticed that they practice shoot-and-release bowfishing, further reducing the already normally low percentage of shad that would return to spawn again.

Another example of shoot-and-release was observed by the writer Jeffrey Cardenas in the vanishingly thin marsh waters of

Lousiana, where redfish often swim with their backs above the surface. There bowhunters go out at night and jacklight redfish from airboats, much as riflemen jacklight deer from cars. The morning after, the flats may be littered with dead and dying fish with gaping arrow holes.

The blunt realities of bowfishing include the problem of what to do with large fish—many of which are held in low esteem—that have holes through them. BowfishTexas.com, operated by a fellow whose boat is named *Killing Spree,* offers advice on this. Suggestions for carp include donating them to a zoo, passing them on to an offshore fisherman for cut bait, or planting them in the ground for fertilizer. He must have had more than a few killing sprees, because he'd already filled all the gardens around his house with dead carp and was now digging up the backyard.

C

CARP BAITS AND ASSOCIATED BRITISH SPECIALIZATIONS

Oversize minnows taken very seriously

To most Americans, the common carp is just that—all too common. Introduced to North America in 1876, with the encouragement of the U.S. Congress, as a means to help feed the growing immigrant population, these deluxe-size minnows were distributed across the continent, flourished, and were mostly ignored. There are few carp aficionados in the United States today, primarily European and Asian immigrants who have carried over their culture's respect for the species, plus a few more established Americans who have discovered that carp aren't all bad. But the majority of U.S. anglers wish they'd simply disappear and stop muddying their favorite trout and bass waters.

The contrast in the perception of carp in Europe could not be more stark. In Britain, France, and other Old World nations today, carp are chased with a level of angling refinement equal to or above that of sophisticated American trout anglers, beginning with bait. Americans are taught to use dough balls—wads of moistened bread. The more dedicated may go the extra step of making concoctions that involve cornbread flour and strawberry gelatin seasoning. But Europeans take their carp baits seriously.

The details of bait preparation fill British carp magazines monthly. Many fishermen rely on maggots, but not all maggots are created equal, those bred in liver being superior. Some anglers cook their maggots on the family stove, this supposedly giving them an attractive "snowy-white appearance" and generating a "very appetising, creamy nutty aroma" in the kitchen. Carp fishers also buy a remarkable array of pellets, particle balls, and groundbaits for attracting and hooking carp, all of which are small man-made balls or crumbs of materials such as peas, hempseed, nuts, groats, breadcrumbs, maize meal, or almost anything else that is edible and can be compacted. Many products make extravagant claims for special nutritive additives that draw the fish, together with flavors as exotic as sweet pineapple, rosehip, Spice'otonic, crab and crawfish, and tutti frutti. But if these formulations aren't potent enough, the baits may be additionally flavored in "booster dips" to try to close the deal.

After casting such a state-of-the-art bait to a likely spot, it's important to detect any subsequent strikes. For this, the European carp angler uses electric bite alarms, which cost about $150 or more apiece, one each for the several rods usually fished at once. The rods are specially designed for the appropriate flex and may reach fourteen feet in length. Patience is required, and the lengthy waits (sessions may be days long) are softened by pitching camp alongside the water. Many anglers sleep in tents, and some have special "bivy" beds for resting outdoors.

Some of the best waters are private stocking ponds that can be fished only for a not-so-nominal fee. To attract carp to the rod, many anglers chum with corn, bait balls, or maggots, using a special slingshot or a baiting spoon, a long-handled spoon that provides leverage for distant flicking, to send the attractants to the desired location. Some anglers even use remote-controlled toy boats, which can cost more than $1,000, to deliver the bait. The angler simply flips a switch from the control box on shore.

The well-equipped carp angler also may own a massive landing net, a weigh sling, an unhooking mat, a sleeping bag, bivy slippers, an antitheft alarm for use while sleeping, a wireless electronic fish finder that is cast from shore, camouflage clothing, tackle luggage, cooking equipment, and a special wheelbarrow for all this gear, at a total cost of many thousands of dollars.

The constant chumming and catch-and-release fishing has yielded some odd results. One is that the fish eat constantly and blow up with huge girths, with relatively short fish achieving great weights. Wild carp are sleek, trim fish; stocking-pond specimens look like puffed-up goldfish. The big fish are so valuable that to purchase one for a pond may cost $1,500 to $2,000. The intensity of the fishery combined with the small size of most of these waters has led to a high degree of familiarity with the fish, and the largest ones are known by name. Open a British carp-fishing magazine, and you'll see numerous photos of a type that shows a sleepy, bedraggled, but smiling Eddie holding horizontally (UK-style) an obese carp named Freddy. Some have become so large and have been caught so many times that they've become nationally famous. The publisher of *Carp Talk*, a British weekly magazine, raised his index finger and bragged to an American reporter, "This is the finger which touched Clarissa."

CAST NETTING

Don't forget to part your jaws

Sometimes what is elegantly uncomplicated conceptually is remarkably difficult to use in practice. For no gear is this more true than for the cast net, which looks effortless when done well but befuddles beginners. A cast net is a circular web with a heavily weighted leadline along its perimeter that is thrown toward and over fish from the shore, dock, or boat. When it is retrieved, the pull of the line gathers the weights into the center of the net, trapping the catch. The technique is straightforward enough, but it's the toss that confounds—a good throw demands two hands, a mouth, and a bit of a dance step.

To throw it, the net should be gathered in both your hands, with part of the leadline held in your mouth. The idea is to sweep your hands in a half-circle motion, as if following through on a baseball bat or golf swing while you step forward. Thrown correctly, the net should open in a graceful swirl to a full circle; a kidney shape is the hallmark of bad form. And if you forget to part your jaws when the leadline flies, you will be forcefully reminded. For those looking for an easier way, a commercially made launcher is now available that looks like an upside-down Frisbee with a handle that is said to be *almost* foolproof.

Most cast netting in U.S. waters today is for small-scale baitfish purposes, but the technique is used in some artisanal commercial fisheries for food fish, such as in the Gulf of Mexico for spadefish. There, fishermen idle close to oil rigs to spot hovering spadefish schools, and then try to throw twenty-four-foot saucers over them. When successful, they retrieve thirty- to forty-pound catches, with a few landing as much as seventy to one hundred pounds.

Worldwide, there are some interesting variations of cast netting. In the Philippines, fishermen leave baited lines in relatively deep water with floats at the surface, not to hook pomfrets, but simply to attract them. They then throw deep-bodied cast nets right

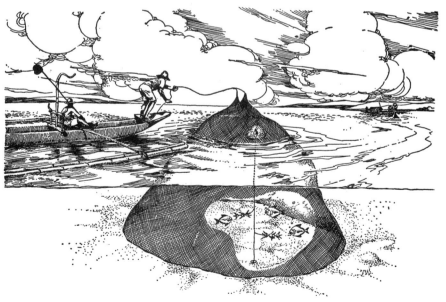

A special deep-water cast net used for catching pomfret in the Philippines.

over the floats to encircle the assembled fish. But before gathering the net, they retrieve the float and line through a special hole engineered at the peak of the net.

A more primitive cast net—one with no central line attached—is used in Asia in the shallows. The fisherman casts the net, which pins the fish in place until he empties it. Another Asian technique is to cast the net over rocky ledges in rivers. The fishermen then spook the fish from their lairs with bamboo poles, and they become entrapped along the rim of the cast net.

Nigerian fishermen of the Lagos Lagoon practice group cast netting. Eight to fifteen canoes, each manned by at least two men, form a circle. The fishermen cast the nets simultaneously, either clockwise or counterclockwise. Sometimes two lines of fishermen face each other and hurl their nets into the intervening area, starting from one end and continuing to the other. In keeping with the cooperative nature of these operations, catches are shared equally among fishermen.

CHAIN AND HOOK

Light-tackle anglers would shudder

Mention Manhattan and sharks together, and high-priced lawyers might spring to mind. But for some time in the 1800s, large sharks were routinely caught in the waters surrounding the heart of New York City. In fact, in 1880 there was a documented attack on a small boat by a group of sharks in the Verrazano Narrows, south of Manhattan Island. The captain fought them off with a wooden seat ripped from the vessel.

Sharks were actively sought by a few practitioners of chain and hook fishing off the piers that lined lower Manhattan. By using a chunk of meat for bait on such primitive tackle, large sharks were caught in surprisingly high numbers, as many as seven in one day. At the foot of Vesey Street along the lower Hudson River is a wood-cutting of a crowd watching a ten-foot shark being hauled onto a dock using a chain and hook, while one man readies a pistol at the fish's head. This phase in Manhattan's history probably occurred because of a much greater number of sharks in the nearshore coastal zone in those days, as well as the poor sanitation of that time, when meat scraps and other food wastes were dumped into adjacent waters, forming an unintended shark-attracting chum slick.

Nowadays in the Big Apple, these sharks are gone, but lawyers still flourish.

CLIFF FISHING

The heights of angling

Ocean cliffs are dramatically rugged landscapes, often towering over fish-rich habitat below them. This has not escaped the attention of adventurous fishermen. Some cliffs may be amenable to climbing part or all of the way to the bottom. Along California's San Mateo coastline, striped-bass anglers clad in wet suits scramble down steep trails or lower themselves on ropes to reach prime casting sites. Even more daring are certain anglers in the Maltese town of Gozo, who dangle from ropes lowered along the cliffs to reach the best, but otherwise, inaccessible, waters.

On the Aran Islands of Ireland, locals fish for wrasse and rockfish off cliffs using three-hundred-foot handlines. To keep the line free from the rock face, the angler extends one leg out and passes the line between his toes. Sensitive digits are needed to detect bites one hundred yards away.

COMMERCIAL LURES OF DUBIOUS VALUE

Some ideas are just too good to work

Ever since the commercial production of American fishing lures began in the late 1800s, the industry has been dominated by the "big five": Heddon, Pflueger, Shakespeare, South Bend, and Creek Chub. But many mom-and-pop outfits, known among collectors simply as the "miscellaneous companies," made particularly unusual lures of dubious value. Maybe that's why they remained the miscellaneous companies.

Around 1920, Abbey and Imbrie sold the Glowbody Minnow, which was filled with a luminous liquid. Two lures were designed to look like a wounded baitfish leaching blood. The Survivor, offered by the Big State Bait Company in the 1930s, had a trapdoor in its belly for inserting blood tablets. The Bleeder, which also was equipped with blood tablets and was modestly advertised as "The World's Greatest Fish Getter," was made in the 1930s and 1940s by—what else—the Bleeding Bait Company.

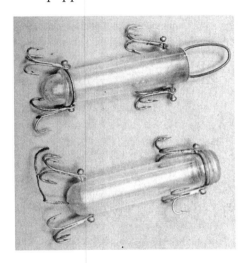

Some lures had a Rube Goldberg quality to them. The Cat's Paw Weedless did not show its hook while being retrieved, but the hook sprang open upon the strike. Many others did this too. Clays Red Head, made in the 1920s, featured an internal spring that allowed the head to pull away from the body when snagged, then snap back, which was meant to free the lure.

The Detroit Glass Minnow Tube, from around 1914, was sort of an aquarium with hooks. The cylindrical glass body was designed to house a live minnow that would draw but be protected from strikes and remain available to catch fish after fish. An alternative approach to the same goal was the Detroit Minnow Bait Cage, a two-hooked minnow-shaped wire lure constructed to hold a

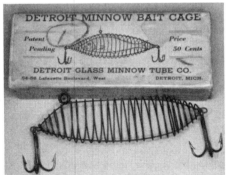

Two lures designed to present a live minnow without sacrificing it: the Detroit Glass Minnow Tube (*top*) and the Detroit Minnow Bait Cage (*bottom*).

live minnow. A crueler device was the Ketchum Frog Gang, a wire harness with hooks designed to stretch out a live frog for trolling. Dubious anglers may have been seduced by the jaunty jingle on the side of the box that read, "A fisherman may fish and a fisherman may lie. What a fisherman can't Ketch a fisherman may buy. No need to lie or buy if you use Ketchum's Patent Frame Gang."

The quaint lures of yesteryear have given way to attractors that are mass-produced by corporations. It's estimated that America's 10.7 million freshwater bass anglers spend about $300 million per year on today's higher-tech artificial lures. The director of one research lab alone has overseen forty thousand experiments designed to better catch fish. Some of the newest lures even ooze shad enzymes to smell like a baitfish.

But other modern commercially available lures are made from simple vernacular objects by what might be termed the miscellaneous companies of today. One fish catcher, conceived and produced by a dentist, is made from a dental dam. Another modern artificial of distinction is the bottle cap lure. Invented in 2000 by a Canadian, the lure is made from a folded beer bottle cap with a swivel, hooks, and ball bearings that rattle around in the fold. Not only has it helped win angling tournaments, but it also provides a use for refuse. Not surprisingly, they may be purchased by the six-pack.

Early and rare commercially made fishing lures are avidly collected and may command remarkably high prices. I recently followed an auction on eBay for a 1909 Chautauqua Minnow in its original box. This shiny, weedless automatic-striking lure is very scarce, and its value was greatly increased by its accompanying container, because original containers are far less likely to survive than the lures themselves. Its owner started the auction at 99 cents. One week and forty-four bids later, the winner of the auction had agreed to pay $45,855, not to mention a few more dollars in postage, because the person auctioning it stated, "Buyer pays all shipping costs."

CORMORANT FISHING

Happy fisherman but frustrated bird

The thirteen-hundred-year-old Asian technique of *ukai*, cormorant fishing for human benefit, survives only as a tourist attraction today, but its uniqueness makes it well worth preserving. Cormorants catch fish by diving underwater, where they swim with agility and grace equal to that of their fish prey. Cormorant fishing is believed to have been invented in the uplands of China, where it was useful in catching fish from narrow, fast-flowing streams. It spread from there and is celebrated in *Manyoshu*, Japan's most ancient poetry anthology, dating to the eighth century. It also was used in Korea and India. Japanese fishermen operated mainly at night with tethered birds under the glow of torchlights, whereas Chinese fishermen worked in daylight with free-swimming birds. Hindus especially appreciated this form of fishing, because their religion prohibits the direct killing of living creatures, but not the eating of fish killed by birds.

Cormorant fishing is still practiced on Japan's Nagara and Li Rivers. It is done at night under the light of torches, usually with twelve feathered accomplices. Much training is involved in preparing cormorants to fish in the service of man, but when accomplished, an individual bird may work for twenty years. The best cormorants are those raised from hatching by the master, who often tends young birds every two to three hours, talking to them and rubbing them gently to make them more tame. The Japanese fisherman, called an *Usho*, manages a flock that may number ten or more. Each cormorant is fitted with a leashlike cord around its neck, which blocks captured fish from passing down its gullet. Once the bird catches a fish, the *Usho* uses a bamboo pole to snare a string tied to the cormorant's legs, then grabs it by the neck and forces it to eject the fish into a bucket.

Military discipline among the cormorants is enforced, with the birds trained to line up in the same order on the edge of the boat. The fisherman also pays attention to their personalities, placing only compatible birds together in transport baskets. When done correctly, tamed cormorants are fishing machines: Efficient birds may catch up to 150 fish per hour.

The cormorants employed around the world were not all of the same species, of which more than two dozen are known to exist. In Japan, four kinds were used, but principally two imported Chinese cormorant species. Whereas in other countries young cormorants had to be caught, the Chinese had great success in breeding them.

Cormorant fishing apparently was introduced into Europe as a sport during the seventeenth century. An image exists of Charles II reclining on a barge, surrounded by young ladies, watching a troupe of trained cormorants catching fish for the party. But the Europeans put a western twist on the technique. Rather than using a leash, they manned the birds as they did hawks, with the bird being trained to fly to the fist. After the cormorant caught a fish, the tender "made in" to the bird, holding out his arm, and then ran his closed hand up the bird's neck, forcing it to regurgitate the fish. The cormorant was rewarded with a minnow small enough to slip past the collar.

Cormorant fishing became quite popular in Europe, especially because it could be practiced during summer, when hawks were molting and couldn't be flown. Louis XIII kept trained cormorants at Fontainebleau and built a series of fish ponds where the birds could display their skills to the king and his court. France's royal keeper of cormorants remained a paid position into the eighteenth century. In England, James I had ponds built at Westminster for his cormorants and trained otters. Cormorant fishing enjoyed a brief revival in the 1800s in England and France, with the French sportsmen going so far as to dress like Chinese mandarins.

In *Fishing from the Earliest Times* (1921), William Radcliffe cites a cruder approach involving cormorants that was practiced on India's Brahmaputra. Wild cormorants would gather midstream and then advance together toward a bank, making a "prodigious pother" by flapping the water with their wings. The panic-stricken fish fled to the shallows and even threw themselves on land. The birds, still in close array, gorged on their penned-in prey. As soon as their feeding ceased, the villagers rushed to the bank and used drums, gongs, and other noisemakers to frighten the cormorants. Too heavy from gorging themselves to fly, the birds had to lighten themselves of most of their meals, which were snatched by the less-than-discriminating peasants.

CREATIVE CHUMMING

The metaphoric dinner bell

Nothing says "come hither" more strongly to hungry fish than free food, which is the underlying theory behind chumming. Chumming is such a fundamental approach that it has been used virtually everywhere fish have been harvested, often with creative twists.

Bluefish in U.S. waters have been chummed by mounting a meat grinder on the stern of a boat and generating a stream of ground menhaden or other baitfish. Nowadays this can be purchased preground in tins from tackle shops. Anglers on headboats out for codfish may be treated to the sight of the boat's mates tossing up and hitting clams fungo-style with baseball bats. This cracks the shell, releasing the juices, and disperses the clams widely around the vessel.

Americans who wish to get chunks of fish down near the bottom in a current sometimes place them in a brown paper tied to a string and weighted with a stone. When deep enough, the angler lifts the line sharply and the bag tears, releasing the chum. In Hawaii, handline fishermen used a similar technique, wrapping a baitfish along with a lava rock and a generous helping of chopped fish in a large leaf. The fisherman wrapped several meters of line around it and tied a slip knot, then dropped it overboard and allowed it to unroll to the desired depth. A tug spilled the contents, which attracted fish to the baited hook.

It's also possible to let commercial fishing operations do the chumming for you. Tuna fishermen worldwide know to look for herring or bottom trawlers pulling up their nets. As this occurs, some smaller fish escape through the mesh, drawing tuna. And when bottom trawlers bring their catch on board, they cull the too-small fish, which sometimes results in a giant chum slick of bite-size fish. Tuna learn to lurk behind and follow these vessels, and tuna anglers have learned to do the same. At Cape Cod, some fishermen shadow commercial vessels that rake sand eels from the bottom; at times, hundreds of stripers can be seen trailing in the clear ocean water. Flounder fishermen in the Northeast use a similar approach, following clammers who rake the bottom, dislodging many benthic invertebrates, including worms, that draw flounder. A related do-it-yourself method is to use a toilet plunger fastened to a long pole to roil up the sediments under a boat.

Europeans use a number of chumming innovations. The English call chum "rubby dubby." One of their methods is to push minced fish into rock crevices at low tide. If the rubby dubby is kept frozen, it will take even longer to disperse. Another simple European approach to chumming for coarse fish is to wrap a ball of ground bait (a kind of mash) around the main bait or sinker, from which it should break off after reaching bottom. The Ukrainians trap their chum against the sinker by using a weight that has a little cage for the chum attached to it. Another chumming device, used in the United Kingdom, is a swim-feeder, a small plastic tube pierced with many holes and fixed with wire rings at each end. The fisherman stuffs it with ground bait and maggots, attaches it above the shot sinkers, and casts it to a likely lie, where it issues its siren aroma. Midwestern American ice fishermen use a related but more elaborate approach. A homemade implement, known as a "chum dumper," is made from PVC pipe with a trigger release and stuffed with bait such as corn or rice.

In the Florida Keys, guides attract sharks by hanging a dead barracuda or two off the boat, the oily scent bringing the great predators within reach of a fly rod. A trick probably used over much of the world is to hang a rotting animal carcass over water so that a stream of maggots falls below. Australians have done this to attract perch and Murray River cod.

Supermarket foodstuffs sometimes make terrific chum. Flounder anglers do well by poking holes in cans of cat food and lowering them to the bottom to release their scent. In Germany, floating dog biscuits attract catfish. Midwestern Americans now routinely chum for catfish using sour soybeans, the nastier the better. A dedicated catfisherman may keep more than a dozen five-gallon buckets in various states of fermentation, with two weeks needed to achieve full ripeness. On a slow day, fifteen gallons of beans may be needed to get the cats biting. Savvy anglers may chum three or four areas before fishing, and then rotate through them later on, reaping the benefits.

An American technique to hold catfish in an area is to place cow pies that have begun to dry in a sack and weight it with rocks. After a suitable period, the sack with now-fermented cow pies is sunk at the head of a major river hole during late spring or early summer—right before catfish spawn. As the fish move upstream to reproduce, they stop below the cow dung chum, and great fishing ensues. But it's not entirely clear whether they hold there because they like the scent or because they dislike it so much that they refuse to swim through it.

One English carp-fishing technique uses a clever chumming approach and catches the fish by snatching. The angler splits the bottom two feet of a long bamboo pole and packs this cavity with material attractive to carp, such as rice and curry. Then he wades out into a carp pond and plunges the stuffed end into the bottom, making sure the other end can be seen above the surface. He backs off and stands by, at the ready with a handline or casting rod rigged with snatch hooks in hand. The pole begins to move when carp are nosing around it, giving away their presence, and a well-placed cast will take them.

Then there is the truly esoteric: Himalayan fishermen use oil from the Ganges River dolphin to attract catfish. Try asking for that at your local tackle shop.

D

DAPPING OR DAPPLING

Wind makes the artificial seem real

Long considered an eccentricity of tweedy, stoic Scots, dapping or dappling is making something of a comeback, even on water bodies whose names don't begin with Loch. Globally, every way in which trout capture food seems to have a fishing technique associated with it. Dapping capitalizes on the tendency for large flying insects to be carried onto lake surfaces on windy days. Trout cruise at some depth below, watching for insects struggling in the surface film. When they spy one, they dart up and take it in a rush.

The dapper has a fishing kit well designed to simulate an unhappy, kicking mayfly, daddy longlegs, or other large terrestrial insect. A bushy fly, or a brace of them—one dark, one light—is fixed on the end of about a twelve-foot length of the traditional embroidery silk or newer polypropylene floss or knotted nylon strands, which is suspended from a thirteen- to fifteen-foot rod. The dapper holds the rod high so that a breeze catches the heavy line and brings life to the presentation. The fly or flies drop onto the water, skitter, and leap, driving the trout below mad. And they see no leader or fly line to give the game away. The beauty of dapping is that the worse the wind is for classic fly casting, the better it is for dapping.

DEEPWATER STURGEON SPEARING

Scraping river bottoms for behemoths

Among the Northwestern tribes, the Coast Salish people specialized in pursuing the giant white sturgeon of the Fraser River, a species that reached twenty feet and eighteen hundred pounds. Harpooning was one of their methods. Sturgeon harpoons could be as long as fifty feet in order to reach the bottom of the holes where the behemoths lay. To allow the fisherman to sense the sturgeon without spooking it, and so that the spear did not have to be raised far to strike, its points were fitted with stiff eagle feathers, which allowed sensitive contact with the substrate. Once a sturgeon was impaled, a line tied to the business end snapped off the shaft bound to the head, so that the fish could be fought off the rope.

Sturgeon spearing on the Fraser River.

"All the Indians now fishing and it is great fun to watch them spearing sturgeon which here run to the great size of 500 and 600 pounds," wrote British Columbia colonial secretary John Birch in 1864. "The Indians drift down with the stream perhaps thirty canoes abreast with their long poles with spear attached kept within a foot of the bottom of the river. When they feel a fish lying they raise the spear and thrust it at the fish seldom missing. The barb of the spear immediately disconnects from the pole but remains attached to a rope and you see sometimes two or three canoes being carried off at the same time downriver at any pace by these huge fish." It could be a long trip. To shorten it, the men dropped heavy stones on cedar bark ropes behind the canoe to steady the craft and to tire the fish out.

Landing the defeated sturgeon was no easy task. Some could be towed back, but other times it was necessary to bring the fish into the canoe—a tricky maneuver that involved tipping the vessel and rolling the fish over the gunwale, then bailing the water out.

Sturgeon behavior changes seasonally, and during summer spawning season, they run shallower. Sometimes the Salish fishermen could spear them at night at depths to eight feet; when the sturgeon swam in more marine waters having bioluminescent microorganisms, the fish's motion would stimulate the little animals to light up. It must have been a remarkable experience to thrust a spear in the dark of night at a glowing ten-foot-long creature from the prehistoric past.

DIP NETTING

Getting the scoop

Dip netting—the gathering of fish with a long-handled net—ranks low on the scale of sophisticated fishing techniques. Yet its success is not a given unless at least one of two conditions exist: The fish must be available near the surface in glutlike abundance, or they must be squeezed through a narrow passage, preferably as they travel against a strong current.

Both considerations were met at the most colorful of dip netting sites—Celilo Falls on the Columbia River, described in Carl Safina's *Song for the Blue Ocean* (1997). This great drainage system once hosted runs of salmon in numbers almost unimaginable today. The falls, nearly one hundred miles from the coast, were visited by Lewis and Clark, who wrote, "Here is the Great fishing-place of the Columbia. In the spring of the year, when the water is high, the salmon ascend the river in incredible numbers." This wealth of food was fished by Native Americans, who built numerous makeshift platforms over the dangerous, roaring rapids, from which they landed huge numbers of salmon. These skilled fishermen mostly

Native Americans dip-netting salmon in the Columbia River at Celilo Falls, Oregon, prior to the damming of the river.

dip-netted, catching as many as twenty large salmon per hour each, but some even speared leaping salmon out of the air.

Constructing the wooden fishing stages also took skill and not just a little daring. The fisherman made holes in the riverbed at some distance from shore to receive the support posts. When the water fell enough during the summer, a strong man was chosen to set the posts. The men pushed a fir sapling out from the bank and sat on it to hold it in place while the chosen man, tied with a safety rope, walked out on it. Carrying a staging pole, the brave soul watched until the swirling water allowed good visibility, dropped one end of the pole into the hole, and then immediately tied it to the fir sapling on which he stood, while those who had remained on shore piled rocks on the sapling's other end. A second post was similarly set, and crossbars were tied between the saplings with hazel ropes. Some netting locations were so isolated that they could be reached only by riding a wicker basket ferry through the air.

The Celilo Falls fishery formed the backbone of a large regional economy and cultural crossroads; indeed, one expert called the tiny fishing community of Celilo Village Oregon's oldest town, with a continuous occupation of at least eleven thousand years. Coastal tribes came not to fish, but to trade whale and cedar products, clams, shells, beads, and canoes; southern peoples brought baskets, obsidian, water-lily seeds, and tobacco; eastern tribes carried buffalo products, pipestone, and feathers. But in the twentieth century, the Columbia was dammed for hydropower, crippling its salmon runs and drowning much of the river. Celilo Falls was submerged in 1957 while Native Americans watched from the banks, some weeping.

A minor but intriguing dip-netting scene was described by Henry David Thoreau in *A Week on the Concord and Merrimack Rivers* (1849). The Connecticut River at Bellows Falls, Vermont, was divided by a great rock island. On the island's steep sides hung several ladders, fastened to armchairs that were secured by a counterpoise. Fishermen sat casually in this odd outdoor living-room scene, dip-netting salmon and shad that passed below.

A truly weird form of dip net was used in New Guinea to skim the surface of the water. An arc of bamboo was fitted with a filtering material made from spiderwebs. Although obviously time-consuming to create, this gear had advantages: These scoops were almost weightless and drained water quickly.

Dip netting is still allowed in parts of Alaska. On the Kenai River during dip-netting season, each Alaskan head of household may catch twenty-five salmon, and families are allotted an additional ten fish per member. When the run is strong, the beach along the lower Kenai becomes a makeshift village of tents, tarps, coolers, and folding chairs. Nearby, in the shallows, a line of dip netters forms, waiting, poised like great blue herons. There is a strange allure to such an unsubtle and direct means of fishing. One first-timer remarked, "It's the most fascinating thing I've ever done. This is only an Alaska thing, it's hard for anybody else to even fathom." But Alaskans find it less mystical; one businesslike Fairbanks native said, "We don't throw 'em back, we don't play with our food."

Dip net spun by spiders on a bamboo frame in New Guinea.

A specialized kind of dip netting takes place in California, as described by John McPhee in *The Founding Fish* (2002). There, delta fishermen capitalize on the spawning behavior of American shad. Shad are not even native to the murky waters of the delta, formed by the confluence of the Sacramento and San Joaquin Rivers. But sometime after shad were carried by train in milk cans from the Hudson River in 1871 and subsequently flourished, fishermen learned that a powerboat with a slowly turning pro-peller somehow simulated a roe shad, thus attracting males. By holding a chicken-wire-meshed dip net alongside the vessel's hull and reacting instantly to the slightest bump, fishermen could scoop mostly male shad. Hence these fishermen are known as "bumpers."

DIVERTING AND BAILING

Subtracting water from the equation

The prehistoric practice of diverting and bailing is so simple that it may strike the modern fisherman as ingenious: Instead of removing the fish from the water that surrounds it, the water that surrounds it is removed from the fish.

This method still is practiced in small ponds in Asia and per-haps elsewhere. Fishermen dig a low ditch up to one shoreline of the water, and then let gravity drain away as much water as possible. Bailing water out of the pond with buckets helps accomplish this goal. After some hours, the now vulnerable fish can be caught with plunge baskets, cast nets, and hand nets. This technique is best performed during dry season, using the head start provided by nature.

Streams are more difficult than ponds for this approach; if the goal is to catch fish by subtracting water, doing so in the endless flow of a stream makes little sense. Diverting the water of a stream is most easily accomplished where two channels pass around an island. Here the fishermen either deflect water into only one channel by building a temporary dam or dig a new diversion channel, causing the water to flow outside of the fishing area. Then they block the partly dewatered fishing channel and hunt the fish in the shallows with the usual assortment of nets, spears, and hands.

DRIVING FISH WITH BIRDS

Feathered border collies

An old European fishing approach is to let wild diving birds drive fish into enclosures. This elaborate technique is based on the efficiency of certain birds at catching fish while swimming underwater. Fish instinctively avoid these hungry predators, and wise fishermen have cleverly harnessed this fear to their advantage.

One location where this method was practiced was Dojran Lake, between what was Yugoslavia and Greece. This circular lake has a nearly uniform depth of ten meters and thus was everywhere accessible to flocks of diving birds, which came from the north to winter there. The fishermen fenced off certain areas of the shallows with grass mats before the migrating birds arrived, leaving only one entrance remaining open toward the lake. Watchmen kept this "safe zone" free from the birds, so that the fish could retreat there once the birds were chasing prey in open water.

To speed the process, the men caught some of the wild birds in traps and clipped their wings. These birds, which were unable to fly, were called "working birds." Most valued were two merganser species, the crested grebe, and one kind each of cormorant and loon. It was important in forming a working group of birds that there be a proper mix of species to create an efficient team.

After several weeks, when sufficient numbers of fish were gathered in the enclosure, the men closed off the entrance with mats. The enclosure was then divided into twenty to thirty chambers, separated from each other by loose mats that allowed fish, but not birds, to pass through. The hungry working birds were introduced to the first chamber, where they would dive after the fish, chasing them into the next available chamber. Any fish too large to pass through the net and be swallowed by the birds—usually carp—were speared by the fishermen.

The men then broke up the now-empty chamber and used the mats elsewhere, as the birds were then allowed into the next chamber. Eventually the fish were tightly corralled in the final chamber, where they were harvested with a funnel-like net. In Dojran Lake, about half of all the fish landed annually were taken with the help of driving birds.

DROP NETTING AND LIFT NETTING

Fishing's ups and downs

Scientists often need to know the density of fish in a given area, but almost all fish capture approaches have issues that make resultant data suspect for comparisons. For example, two apparently identical trawl nets might catch fish at different rates when pulled behind two different vessels. In an effort to have a simple method of estimating fish abundance at a single site over different time periods, the drop net was invented.

A drop net operates among a set of pilings in the water. The bottom of the drop net is weighted with a chain, and a line is connected to the chain at each piling. Each line then passes through a pulley at the top of each piling above the surface of the water. When the lines are pulled taut, the net is clear of the water, but when the lines are suddenly released, the net plummets to the bottom, trapping any fish present below.

Lift net fished off stilts in Philippines rivers to catch mullet.

Lift nets are the conceptual opposites of drop nets. The idea is to suddenly lift fish straight up and out of the water. These exist in many variations worldwide. The simplest is used by anglers to catch baitfish. The fisherman drops a yard-wide umbrella net off a pier and throws sardine pieces or other kinds of chum above it, waits until minnows or silversides are seen, then lifts sharply. But heavy counterbalanced lift nets many square yards in size are used off boats and barges, as are lift nets that are stretched between both banks of a river. Some lift nets are so large that they are brought to the surface by ships, each of which tows one of its four ends.

DYNAMITE AND OTHER KINDS OF BLAST FISHING

Sometimes necessary, always wasteful

Dynamiting is a somewhat less-than-subtle approach, but it will provide fish for the table, not to mention a substantial charge of excitement. Not surprisingly, it was said to be Saddam Hussein's favorite fishing technique. There exists a strange film of the dictator wearing a long coat and beret, lobbing a grenade into the water, underhanded, with aides in scuba gear gathering his "catch."

Not everyone feels morally or environmentally, not to mention legally, comfortable tossing a lighted stick of TNT into the water. For a while a joke was making the rounds of the fisheries world: Joe invited his friend Sam to go fishing with him on his boat. They motored to the spot, and instead of casting his rod, Joe took out a dynamite stick, lit it, and threw it a safe distance away. It exploded underwater, and soon fish littered the surface. Sam was shocked and screamed, "What are you doing? This is wrong!" To which Joe replied by handing Sam another lighted dynamite charge and saying, "Are you going to talk or are you going to fish?"

During World War II, GIs in the South Pacific were known to use hand grenades, the "soldier's fishhook," to catch fish. They'd lob a charge to a likely spot among the coral, wait for the blast, and soon fish bobbed all over. One time a destroyer was getting low on food, but the captain could not ask for permission to fish, inasmuch as it is not part of naval protocol. So the captain asked for approval to perform an antisubmarine exercise with the squids—squid-shaped depth charges that are launched well ahead of the ship. A school of fish was located and the squids launched, with the catch rounded up in a man-overboard exercise.

In some places around the world, "fishermen" create their own explosives. During World War II, the Japanese government put Palauans to work fishing to help feed Japan's troops. There were many more Japanese than Palauans, however, and most Palauan canoes and rafts had been destroyed for security reasons. But dynamite provided by the Japanese provided a solution. Fish bombs were made by packing beer cans about two-thirds full with gunpowder. The fuse was made from match head shavings tamped into a thin bamboo rod, stuck into the powder, and sealed with mangrove mud. A clever adjustment was to vary the length of the bamboo rod so that the bomb would explode at the appropriate depth for the type of fish being sought.

Blast fishing in the Philippines also arose from events of World War II. Talisay Beach was the site of fierce fighting between resisting Japanese soldiers and American liberators. Among the battle-field debris littering the beach after the war were large deposits of unspent munitions and gunpowder. Local residents, perhaps having seen during the war the effects on fish of bombs exploding offshore, began to use the beach as a laboratory for manufacturing explosives. These homemade bombs worked so well that a market developed for them in other towns and provinces. In the Philippines, a nitrate-based fertilizer, in powder form, is still commonly used. It is mixed with gasoline or methyl alcohol, and the product is poured to the brim in soft-drink or other kinds of glass bottles. The bottle is then topped with a blasting cap or detonator and sealed with candle wax.

Catching fish by blasting is the antithesis of sustainable fishing; not only does this short-sighted approach cause many useful fish to sink to the bottom with ruptured gas bladders, but it also causes enormous damage to the habitat, especially coral reefs, which reduces fish production for future generations. When a hand grenade was exploded experimentally, a diver brought up ten times as many fish from the depths as were gathered on the surface.

E

EEL FISHING'S MANY VARIATIONS

Unusual fish, unusual fishing

Eels, with their snakelike bodies and slick, slime-covered skin, present a unique set of obstacles—but also many unusual options—for their capture. Many may wonder, why bother? Today the typical American reaction to eel consumption is "Ugh!" But eels were widely harvested for food in earlier generations. Colonists sometimes ate them *spitchcocked*—arranged in a circle head to tail and roasted. They were so commonly eaten in the Northeast in the 1830s that New Englanders were referred to as "Eels" in the same way Indianans were nicknamed "Hoosiers." Eels still are caught commercially in North America for certain ethnic groups that enjoy them; as bait, mainly for striped bass; and as tiny juveniles for export to the Japanese market, where they will be grown to marketable size.

But the sublime taste of eels is still widely appreciated elsewhere in the world. Eels are so esteemed in Sweden that there is an event named an *alagille,* in which eels are cooked six or more ways, including in soup, fried, grilled over linden wood, boiled, baked, or smoked. At an *alagille,* copious vodka helps the eel go down, and the first man to eat enough eel portions to line the edge of his plate with eel spines is declared the eel king.

Eels of different kinds occur in all of the temperate oceans, and they share similar and remarkable life histories, kind of the opposite to salmon. The American eel is spawned in the depths of the Sargasso Sea, in the lower latitudes of the North Atlantic Ocean. Its eggs and transparent larvae drift for half a year or more in the Gulf Stream before the "glass eels" move shoreward to invade estuaries and rivers. There, they darken and transform into "elvers," which are miniature adults. Eels mature as "yellow eels" along the coast or in brackish or fresh waters (some swim as far inland as tributaries to Lake Superior) for as long as twenty-five years before transforming to big-eyed "silver eels," which migrate all the way back to the Sargasso Sea to spawn and die. Other eel species use comparable currents to the Gulf Stream in their ocean regions to disperse their young.

It's awfully hard to physically hold a squirming eel. The "eel grip," with the middle finger around the fish's body and the adjoining fingers bracing the other side, usually holds for only seconds before the eel slides in one direction or the other. But metaphysically, the Japanese hold eels in high regard. In the eighth century, a Japanese poet advised a thin friend thus: "Let me tell you, Imawaro, that you should eat an eel, which they say is good for you after you have lost weight through the heat of the summer." This notion still prevails, with the eel considered an excellent source of vitamins and nutrients. With their widespread distribution, delicate flavor, and unique morphology and habits, eels have a long history of capture via myriad specialized approaches.

Oppian, in his *Halieutica* (A.D. 180), wrote of a probably apocryphal but not impossible approach, in which an eeler from a high bank of the "river Eretaenus, where the eels are the largest and by far the fattest of all eels," let down at the turn of the stream a length of sheep intestines. An eel, seizing its other end, tried to make off with it, at which time the fisherman blew into a long, tubular reed fastened to the organ's other end. The intestines swelled; the fish, receiving air in his mouth, swelled too, and unable to extricate its teeth, was hauled out, affixed to the inflated intestines.

A Japanese eel-fishing technique capitalized on the fish's predilection to swim into and occupy small cavelike structures.

Two-foot-long bamboo tubes four inches in diameter were sunk long enough for eels to inhabit them before they were retrieved. Public aquariums often place pipes as homes for eels in their tanks, but they make sure they are short enough that the eels must keep their heads visible to viewers. Old Chesapeake Bay eel traps were made of wooden splints to form round, elongated baskets with internal splint funnels that guides the hungry eels to the bait but discouraged their exit. More simply, it's not unusual to find them in the water-filled rims of automobile tires in the intertidal zone of beaches.

Nepalese fishermen catch eels with brush traps that attract them as hideouts. The fishermen place brush bundles assembled from about two hundred twigs in swampy areas with high numbers of eels. To create a sheltering den inside and to sink the bundle, stones are placed in the middle of it. The eel "home" is covered with wet leaves to make it even more enticing, and then it is left overnight. Early in the morning, the brush-bundle fisherman carefully approaches the bundle, and then lifts it and tosses it on shore in one motion. If too many eels to handle begin to squirm out of the pile, the fisherman throws a cast net over it to keep them from escaping.

Eels have long been impaled with an awesome variety of hand-forged spear designs, many of which exhibit a graphic union of form and function and are avidly sought by collectors. Some designs used in the nineteenth century reach as far back as ancient Egypt, four millennia ago, when they were reproduced as hieroglyphics. Summer spears were engineered to nab free-swimming eels, usually visually and sometimes by the light of a torch, and consequently were meant to connect with the fish on the downward stroke. An English glaive, or greave, was an ornate sand or hard-bottom summer spear. Used in the fen country of East Anglia, these spears had blunt tips but serrated notches between the tines to wedge the eels in place. Europeans also used eel combs— fine-toothed rakes that could be drawn through the muck.

Winter spears take advantage of the habit of eels to bury in mud during cold periods. To be able to be "raked" at an angle through good bottom, their poles were usually fourteen to sixteen

Part of a remarkable collection of antique eel spears.

feet long, and sometimes as much as twenty feet long. In order to snatch the eels from their burrows, winter spears have upward-facing barbs at the ends of their six or eight ten-inch-long tines. Because of the small market for this gear in the United States, eel spears of this kind were forged by local makers; those with makers' marks are valuable antiques today. A good spear was cherished. It had to have a central "knife" to withstand the brunt of the blow when the spear was jabbed into the bottom, yet the tines had to be limber enough to spring back when an eel or branch was removed.

Years ago, I was fortunate to witness a winter eel fishery on an ice-covered bay on Long Island Sound, where this once common activity is now rarely practiced. The fishermen made several two-foot holes in the ice. This seemed like a small window to the bottom below, but by using a very long pole and raking with a snatching motion in a wide radius, a great deal of mud was sieved. Before long, the old-timers had a remarkable number of dark eels lying sinuously, numbed, against the white ice. I'm not sure how much they weighed, but long ago a Cape Codder reported average catches of thirty to forty pounds per eeler, and when a great bed was found, as much as several hundred pounds.

An old-fashioned approach used in North America and Europe is called bobbing (in some places babbing, and in Germany, *naring*), originated so long ago that it appears in the *Oxford English Dictionary* of 1660. When bobbing, up to about one hundred worms are strung lengthwise on a cotton or wool thread and then wound in a coil of almost a foot in diameter, to which a small sinker may be added. The rig is fished vertically off a pole or handline. When the angler feels nibbles along with additional weight, he swings the line gently upward onto the boat, dock, or shore, with the eels attached, having gotten their teeth snagged in the worsted twine. A similar approach is used in the Delaware River, and perhaps elsewhere, with worms stuffed into little weighted sacks made from old nylon stockings. The eels bite and their teeth become snagged. Because the eels are not actually hooked, it's important to have a way to secure them immediately. On his first time out, one angler swung four eels at once onto a sloping bank, but he and his brother and two dogs were all unable to grab them, all four eels reentering the water with the dogs right behind them.

Another traditional eel-fishing technique is sniggling. The sniggler takes a bent stick and ties a line between it and the eyed half of a darning needle. A worm is impaled on the other half of the needle, and the point is stuck into the bent end of the stick. This business end is then placed by holes and crevices that are likely to hold eels. When an eel seizes the worm, it dislodges the needle from the stick. The sniggler allows a minute or two for the eel to engulf the worm. Then, when the line is pulled, the needle lodges sideways in the fish's throat, as a gorge.

Eels have a propensity for entering the body cavities of carcasses and then feeding inside. Shad fishermen who leave their gill nets soaking for too long in New York's Hudson River have been known to see fat eels full of shad roe squirm out of the big herring's abdominal cavities. In Europe, an eel trap was sometimes made from a hollowed sheep carcass that was sealed shut except for a small neck opening.

The Irish used an eel-fishing method that seems downright perverse, in that they would gaff swimming or resting eels, which is kind of like gaffing spaghetti. Moreover, the smaller the eel, the more difficult the target. But with a fine eel switch, a good catch could be gathered. An eel switch was made of a long, thin gaff stick, on one end of which was lashed a knitting needle, and tied to that was a codfish hook. An eel switcher would drift silently over a lake on a calm day, kneeling on the bottom of the boat until he saw an eel. Then he slowly lowered the switch until it was within an inch or two of the eel's body. He gave a sudden jerk, and up would come a writhing, astonished eel. The best switchers could also nab eels at night with the aid of a torch and even take an occasional trout.

The eel rack—a passive approach to capturing silver eels migrating downstream in rivers—is still used in a few locations, such as the Delaware River in New York. The eel fishers begin with long, V-shaped walls of stone laboriously built across a river's flow during low water in summer. At the point of the weir is built a wooden contraption on stilts, the body of which is composed of a series of stairlike sections of slats about ten feet wide and five feet long, with the individual slats spaced about a half inch apart. Each of these sections is called a fall. The downstream end is about ten inches higher than the upstream end, and thus the falls lead up out of the water, with one fall always in the water. The beauty of this system is that if the river rises or drops, one of the falls is always working.

As eels swim downstream, the V-shaped weir forces them over the falls and strands them in the one fall that has the least amount of water. They can't go forward because there is no water, and they can't go back upstream because the slats of each fall project like a shelf over them. Often the operators can simply come at their leisure to remove the catch, but on dark and rainy nights, the eels may accumulate at such a pace that they must rake, carry, and store eels all night long.

Rack used to catch eels migrating to sea on the Delaware River, New York.

Eels are remarkably tolerant of pollution and are often found in the aquatic interstitial spaces of cities. It may or may not be an urban legend, but it's been said that during London's siege in World War II, residents fished for eels at night by lifting up manhole covers and dropping baited lines into sewers. This is not farfetched, as an acquaintance of mine once saw a man catching eels from a sewer hole on a Manhattan street using an upside-down umbrella.

EEL SKIN PLUGS

A sack of skin comes to life

Along the New England and mid-Atlantic coasts, serious anglers know that large striped bass—and to a lesser degree, bluefish and weakfish—like to eat live eels. But especially for surf casters, it's not easy to carry living eels around while walking and wading in the harsh environment of pounding waves. Moreover, live eels are not always readily available, and they don't cast well.

One elegant solution that was popular during the mid-1900s, but has since fallen out of favor except by a hard-core few, is casting eel skin plugs. These are wooden fishing lures that are fitted with skins of eels, the marriage resulting in a presentation that casts well, is always available once made (and cared for), and smells and looks like an eel, its motion stemming from the swimming action of the lure.

But making and maintaining eel skin plugs take considerable effort. To prepare the eel skin, it's best to nail a dead eel through its skull to some solid piece of wood. Make a circular cut just below the head, and pull the skin off as if it were a sock. This turns the skin inside out, revealing an attractive blue coloration that fishes well. Slide the skin over a plug from which you have removed the hooks, making sure that a generous length of skin hangs behind the lure. Then tie the skin down near its front end using fine wire, string, or rubber bands. Make small cuts in the skin where the hooks were, reattach them, and the rig is ready to be fished. Some matches of skin and lure work better than others. A good one can be magical, as that long tail undulates with all the allure of a live eel, if not more.

ELECTROFISHING

A shocking practice

Touch a short-circuited wire, and you know the power of electricity to incapacitate. Run current through a fish, and it too will be stunned. But electrofishing is a specialized practice, usually performed by researchers (or poachers), in habitats where netting is difficult. Because salt water is so conductive, the electrical current tends to flow around fish instead of through them, making electrofishing ineffective in marine environments. But electrofishing's efficiency in fresh water can be astounding. There are many accounts of researchers shocking rivers thought to be "fished out," only to turn up dozens to hundreds of trout.

Electrofishing is practiced in streams using backpack units, or in deeper waters from specially rigged boats. In both cases, additional participants beyond the unit operator are needed to scoop stunned fish before they recover. Electricity may be produced on-site using generators or stored in batteries. Accidental shocks while electrofishing can be painful, so it's important to wear rubber waders or other appropriate safety gear. While in graduate school, I went stream shocking with my advisor, who was working an old backpack shocker. It was great fun to try to dip-net the many trout and minnows that turned up, the several graduate students vying for specimens like hockey players on a face-off. Unfortunately, the unit had a short circuit, and every time my advisor released the charge, his shoulder convulsed; this fishing required more than the usual dose of stoicism.

The effectiveness of electrofishing varies greatly with the equipment and circumstances. Larger electrodes produce larger stun fields. The mineral content of the water also affects electrical field size. Bony fish—which include most species—conduct electricity better than cartilaginous fish, such as sharks and lampreys. Larger specimens sustain more total body voltage than smaller individuals in the same field. AC and DC currents cause different muscular responses by fish, with pulsed rather than continuous DC offering the best combination of potency and efficiency. Moderate currents are necessary to stun them. Too much electrical current will kill fish (AC may cause contractions so severe as to break the vertebral column), and too-low currents will allow them to escape. However, it's not true that electroshocking will cure a fish's psychosis.

A fish reacts to a suitable DC current in three discernible stages. When a fish enters the electrical field, it feels the first stage of agitation; some may react by fleeing. The second stage is galvanotaxis, in which the fish is drawn to the anode. When the fish nears the anode, the third stage, narcosis, occurs; this is when the fish sinks and must be caught.

Wild fish are notorious for not cooperating when you need them to, such as when you're showing off a new spot to a friend or displaying a fishery to visitors. But the brute force of electrofishing can overcome that. During a conference on sturgeon in Oshkosh, Wisconsin, a field trip was planned to view lake sturgeon on the Fox River. The choreography was Broadway quality. Buses discharged dozens of international sturgeon researchers on a highway bridge, from which nothing could be seen below the river surface. Everyone milled around, wondering why the group had been brought to such a mundane spot. Suddenly a flotilla of electrofishing boats run by the state of Wisconsin appeared around the bend. As they neared the bridge, the electrical fields turned over nearly a dozen beautiful sturgeon, a forced cooperation on their part that had the crowd enraptured.

Believe it or not, recreational electrofishing is legal on parts of the Cape Fear River in North Carolina, and other states are considering legalizing it. Of course, illegality doesn't stop committed poachers from doing this throughout the South and Midwest. The basic apparatus of the North Carolinian recreational electrofisher is a homemade cranker. A cranker usually is made with a hand-crank telephone magneto generator that produces less than seventy-five volts at one-half to one ampere. The generator is connected to wire electrodes suspended from a boat to the bottom. Using a cranker has also been called "monkey fishing" because it reminds practitioners of old-time organ grinding, which traditionally occurred with a monkey present. Another kind is the Skoal can shocker, housed in a tobacco tin. A series of resistors and diodes are placed in the tin and powered by a twelve-volt battery. Practitioners drift down the river and dip the disoriented fish as they arc to the surface.

These various homemade shockers work well and are amenable to poaching. Recently in Florida, where shocking remains illegal, a conservation officer found several guys with thirty-one flathead catfish, three blue cats, and two channel catfish in the bottom of their boat, along with a dip net. After some discussion, they produced a Mongomery Ward electric fence charger modified to shock fish. A Georgia poacher bragged how his homemade unit delivers big flatheads, yet cost only $6 in parts from Radio Shack.

The stakes—and the voltages—are higher in Russia, where poachers seek sturgeon for valuable caviar. There the fishermen use commercial electroshocking equipment, but they crank the power up so high that the sturgeon's eyes explode, and anything alive in the field, even plankton, is killed.

The joy of illicit shocking was demonstrated recently in Florida, where a warden arrested two Ocala brothers in the same area where he had caught them previously twenty-five years earlier, but not in between. When they were cited, one of the brothers told him he'd had a heart attack the year before and had to have one more go at it before he died.

But maybe making it legal is the best way to reduce its use. A colleague of mine who talked with local North Carolina crankers was told, "It was a lot more fun when it was illegal."

F

FISH HOUSES, ON THE ICE AND OTHERWISE

A little northern comfort

Portable fishing houses are part of the landscape in high-latitude areas that provide long ice-fishing seasons. In a few places, they form a major part of the landscape. On Mille Lacs Lake in Minnesota, every winter a temporary village materializes, made up of as many as twenty thousand people and fifty-five hundred fish houses, a population larger than 90 percent of the state's towns that exist on actual soil. So intensively is the lake fished that roads are plowed and road signs mounted on the ice, speed limits are posted, trash is picked up, and pizza is delivered.

Most of the ice houses on Mille Lacs are individually owned, but some are rented, with transportation out to the ice provided. Ice houses may be spartan cubicles, or they may contain some combination of gas heaters, cookstoves, refrigerators, tables, chairs, bunks, carpeting, insulation, paneling, thermal windows, curtains, lighting, bathrooms, televisions and antennas, and music systems. In fact, there are persistent rumors of fish houses on Mille Lacs with large-screen satellite TVs, digital satellite dishes, and even hot tubs.

Fish houses for use on the ice are so popular in the upper Midwest that they've been extended for use on liquid water. On Wisconsin's Wolf River, fish houses on small barges are arrayed tight to the bank at strategic spots for walleye fishing on the spring spawning run. Numerous rod holders are mounted along the outside railing, and the angler can watch the baited rods placed in them from a large window inside the house, which is outfitted with many amenities. When a strike occurs, an angler can put down his coffee and be fighting a fish in seconds.

Despite the sometimes brutal weather conditions, the dedication of ice fishermen can be remarkable. A few years ago on Lake Simcoe in Ontario, anglers were fishing when a gap opened in the ice, spreading quickly until it was more than one hundred yards wide and twenty miles long. Six military helicopters, a hovercraft, and several boats rescued several hundred fishermen, but high winds and snow suspended the rescue at nightfall, leaving two hundred people stranded on the ice. The next day, eighty-three more people were brought to shore, but dozens of others insisted on staying. One policeman summed up the situation with this observation: "They're determined ice fishers."

FISH WHEELS

Sometimes circular reasoning pays off

From a distance, a fish wheel looks a lot like a paddleboat anchored in a river. But get closer and you'll see an ingenious device that catches fish as its wheel revolves in the current. The use of a fish wheel is passive fishing at its finest. Net baskets turn by water power as if seats on a Ferris wheel, trapping fish as they sieve through the flow, and then, as they rotate, dropping the catch onto a slide and into a holding pen. The contraption generates a whole lot of impressive mechanical activity and large catches, and the fisherman doesn't even have to be there.

Fish wheels normally are supported by a scow or pontoons. They are set at strategic locations and kept in place with anchors or posts, sometimes with lead nets to steer fish toward the apparatus. The trick to rigging a fish-gobbling wheel is to figure out the most effective number of revolutions per minute. One wheel on British Columbia's Fraser River fished best when it completed a turn every twenty-four seconds. A working fish wheel makes a steady *plink, plink, plink* noise over the river's natural hum as the basket's cross braces strike the water.

Fish wheels may have been invented in China and have also been employed in Japan, in France on the Garonne, and in Rome on the Tiber. They were first used in the United States in North Carolina in 1829. But their major deployment has been on the West Coast, where they have been highly effective at landing upstream-migrating salmon. Fish wheels appeared on the Columbia River by 1879, but they later were the target of antagonism by the general public, owing to their supposedly destructive powers, and they were banned for commercial fishing in 1926 in Oregon and 1934 in Washington. Wheels operating at prime locations bordering rapids at the Cascades and The Dalles—sites of huge dams today—plucked as much as thirty million tons of salmon from the Columbia each year. A full-sized replica of the 1881 McCord fish wheel, once used near the present-day Bonneville Dam, is an attraction at the Columbia Gorge Interpretive Center.

But although today fish wheels can't be used commercially in many places in North America, they are ideal for researchers monitoring fish populations, because their catches aren't harmed and thus can readily be measured, weighed, tagged, and released. They also are not species-selective; one fish wheel's daily harvest in October on the Fraser River system in British Columbia included 4 sockeye salmon, 186 chum salmon, 36 chinook salmon, 505 coho salmon, 3 steelhead, and 1 sturgeon.

Fish wheels may be making a comeback as a commercial fishing technique. Large rivers often host runs of several kinds of salmonids, some of which may be plentiful and others reduced. Many alternative gear types, such as gill nets, kill much of what is caught. But because fish-wheel catches are kept alive in holding pens, they may be sorted, with protected fish released unharmed. Also, the quality of the harvested fish is first-class, as they are not damaged by netting and can be kept alive until sent to fish processors.

Because using fish wheels to catch spawning salmon going upstream works so well, someone had the idea of using wheels for research purposes to catch their young, known as smolts, moving downstream. Thus the smolt wheel was born. Smolt wheels look like the casing of a turbine on a jet plane. Inside the wheel is a series of baffles that capture smolts and drop them into a pen, where they pause before being counted and released on their way to the sea.

Fish wheels became popular in Alaska since they were introduced by gold stampeders around 1900, and they are still used by subsistence fishermen today, especially in winter to catch food for sled dogs. Anyone interested in owning one can find toy models in Alaskan gift shops.

FOOT FISHING FOR FLATFISH (AND ROUNDFISH)

Keeping a plaice in place

Foot fishing is practiced worldwide wherever the lower extremities can assist the upper ones, but it is especially popular in Europe. In the United Kingdom, keeping a plaice in place with one's foot before it can be picked up by hand is known as "treading flukes." In France, this oft-practiced technique is called *pêche à pied*. And on the East Frisian North Sea coast, the taking of turbot from pools that remain as the tide ebbs is named *buttpetten*.

Foot fishing for flatfish is simple. Wade slowly into a river inlet or shallow bay with bare feet. When your foot slides over a flounder, simply step down hard to pin it, then reach down and grab it and bag it. Sometimes distinct pools are worked together by a line of a half dozen people. Accomplished treaders can fill a sack this way, but it may not be for the ticklish.

Native Americans of the Pacific Northwest coast also foot-fished for partially buried flounder on mudflats or sandbars, but they used spears to secure the fish, as do the Welsh. In the Welsh technique, the barefoot fisherman works upcurrent, feeling for the flounder's tail. The flounder spooks and turns to escape downstream, giving a moment to strike—with luck in the fish's tail and not in the spearer's toes. Some English treaders also use spears. The fisherman feels the flounder with his bare foot, then reaches down and strokes his hand up the fish's back before poking the spear through its head.

A foot-fishing technique that is truly elegant in its simplicity is practiced in the Danish part of Vadehavet—the shallow waters on the west coast of Denmark, Germany, and the Netherlands. There, on low tide, fishermen walk the flats with no hope of catching flounder at that time. But they come back on the rising tide, stepping into their own footprints for flounder that have come to rest in those depressions.

Feet may also be used for more typically shaped "roundfish." In modern Egypt, fishermen use their toes and soles to feel for the spawning holes of tilapia. Once a hole is located, the foot fisher grabs the nest-guarding female by hand.

Even more esoteric is to walk on hard earth to find fish below. Lungfish burrow into the mud as their water dries up seasonally. But fishermen can locate them by stamping on the baked mud and then dig them out by hand or with hoes.

FROST FISHING

Fish that land themselves

Although this rarely occurs nowadays because of their seriously depleted stocks, the normally deep-dwelling silver hake often chased baitfish in to shore at dusk or at night. Being unaccustomed to skinny water, it was not unusual for the hungry hake to run right up onto the sand. I witnessed this phenomenon in New York one May as silver hake filled the shallows, with a few flinging themselves on shore. But it most frequently occurs during winter, often enough in the old days that it was given the name "frost fishing." Sometimes the frost fish were already frozen solid when found, ready for long-term storage.

FRUIT TREE FISHING

Rising water + falling fruit = large catches

Many tropical rivers experience seasonal flooding, but nowhere as pronounced as in the Amazon River basin of South America, where water levels may rise thirty to forty feet and surge nearly twenty miles inland. Here the drowned forest is known as *varzea.* A forest that becomes flooded offers challenges and opportunities for wildlife. Terrestrial animals must go up—ascending to higher terrain or climbing up trees. But now fish suddenly can swim among the tree trunks. Many of the trees have evolved to drop their fruit and seeds during high water to better disperse them. And many fish that invade these areas are herbivorous, having evolved to capitalize on the abundance of fruit and seeds.

The tambaqui is a large fish that crushes fallen seeds with its strong jaws. These fish often gather beneath trees bearing the seeds they prefer, a fact that fishermen use to their advantage. Some elongated and flattened fruits characteristic of the legume family hang over rivers in South America; these fruits ripen and explode, with fish gathering underneath to eat the seeds. Indians think the fish hear the fruit explode, others are convinced it's the sound of the vibrations from the fruit hitting the water, and still others believe the fish sticks its snout out of the water to sniff the odors of ripening fruit. According to Amazonian folklore, jaguars prey on herbivorous fish by listening for the thud of falling seeds. Others claim that the jaguar crouches on a branch over the water and taps the surface to imitate falling fruit, to draw tambaqui and other fish near.

To catch tambaqui and other herbivorous fishes, native fishermen feign falling fish food. In Brazil, fishermen use a *gaponga,* a weight tied to the end of a line and pole, repeatedly dropping it on the river surface to imitate the sound of falling fruit. Fishermen spear the fish that are attracted with the expectation of finding—rather than being turned into—a meal.

G

GAFFING

The artful lift

The gaff, a large hook on the end of a pole, is most often associated with landing large fish subdued by other means. When an angler has the tired quarry boatside, it can be lifted aboard after impaling it with a gaff hook. Some fish are too large and dangerous for a standard gaff; they may zoom off, pulling the gaffer along for a ride if he doesn't let go. The flying gaff was created for such occasions. Here the hook disengages but is secured by a cable, and the angler fights the fish once again, but with sterner gear.

Fishermen have used gaffs to catch fish in the rivers of the Himalayas for millenia; in fact, some believe that method—essentially an extension of man's grasp—is the earliest fishing technique. Gaff hooks mounted on long poles were held vertically until a large fish was seen or felt, and then snatched upward.

There are other situations where gaffs are used directly to catch fish. In the Amazon, fishermen use barbed gaffs during flood periods to catch catfish swimming upstream along its banks. During low water, fishermen build platforms along the shores. Then, when waters rise, they stand on the platforms and stroke their eighteen- to thirty-foot-long gaffs up and down until they hook a fish.

Miniature gaffs have been used to collect toadfish, which are cave dwellers. When scientists in Central America had trouble gathering them, children made gaffs from coat hangers, and then dove near the toadfish's hideouts and pulled them out by jabbing their little gaffs into the corners of the fish's mouths.

GAS BALLOONING

Up high Down Under

Balloons have been used sporadically as fishing tools for some time, with the sphere usually riding directly on the water surface. An old trick for catching walleye was to attach a balloon on a long, fine line to the first one caught, and then release it to rejoin its school. By following the balloon, many more walleye could be landed.

Ballooning achieved new heights with the addition of helium gas. This approach has reached a sophisticated level on the forty- to one-hundred-foot volcanic cliffs of Quobba Station in western Australia. There the desert meets the ocean at dangerous rocky

Gas ballooning gear.

precipices, and large game fish cruise just offshore. Following the lead of a creative Australia Meteorological Bureau employee presumably familiar with weather balloons, anglers now carry helium gas tanks to the cliffs. There they use them to fill large toy balloons to carry their offerings far out over the waves on the strength of easterlies that prevail at certain times of the year. The fishing is dangerous; someone is lost every year or two, and others are swept away but make it back. But the incentives are strong: A day's catch may consist of several bluefin tuna, cobia, and a local wahoolike species, among others.

Fighting a game fish from an ocean cliff.

A fine Australian mackerel landed while gas ballooning.

Bait or lures may be fished with helium balloons. To present either properly, a seventy-five-yard length of line tied to the balloon is attached to a six-foot leader in front of the offering. Because of the possibility of truly large sharks, cobia, tuna, and even billfish, heavy tackle with up to almost a thousand yards of line is used. Fish may have to be dragged over ledges below before they are in a position to be gaffed. Anglers use sectional pole gaffs as long as thirty-five feet or "cliff gaffs" made of sash cord and hooks. This technique is productive for species that anglers usually need a large offshore fishing boat to catch, and the height allows the angler to witness many savage strikes.

Fishing with breath-filled balloons is practiced creatively elsewhere. On one U.S. lake, the idea is to use the balloon get the rig way out, and then have the terminal tackle drop to the bottom. To accomplish this, anglers attach balloons to the main line using Life-savers candies, which eventually dissolve, freeing the line to descend. But if you try this, choose your candies carefully; mint-flavored Lifesavers do not last as long as the hard candies in the assorted pack.

GATHERING SPAWNERS ON THE BEACH

Could it be any easier?

Some fish have evolved remarkable breeding behaviors, including spawning on land, which served them well until humans began picking them up in the act. The most famous of these is California's grunion runs. Grunion are small, smeltlike fish that on certain nights leap onto the shore in droves, where people often are waiting to meet them, flashlights and buckets in hand. How do they know the grunion will appear?

Actually, few fish are more predictable in their habits. Long observation has shown that grunion spawn at night shortly after high tide, but only during the second, third, and fourth nights following the full moon in March, April, May, and June. It is a well-choreographed event. Like surfers, pairs of grunion ride the crests of the waves onto the beach. When the wave flattens on shore, the pair swims onward, pushing through the succeeding wave. Then the female digs her tail into the sand and the male arches himself across her, and they spawn quickly before riding the next receding wave back out to the sea. Two weeks later, the eggs hatch and the larvae emerge on the equally high new-moon tides.

Grunion runs last for only a few hours, but thousands may be on the beach at once, making the gathering easy. Grunion are delicious, and parties are often held on the beach, with grunion skewered in bonfires.

A similar fish, capelin, performs a comparable ritual in parts of the Canadian Maritimes. In Newfoundland, the capelin run in summer, and their presence often corresponds with a sudden influx of whales and seabird mobs that feed on them. When capelin hit the beach, they can turn the shores spongy with their reddish spawn, which may reach a foot deep in places. Capelin are gathered by the bushel to be fried, smoked, salted, or used as fertilizer.

GILL NETS AND TRAMMEL NETS

Swimming into walls

Gill nets are so familiar in many parts of the world that the beauty of their fundamental design is perhaps taken for granted. A gill net essentially is a vertical wall of mesh webbing that catches fish that attempt to swim through it. As the fish drives forward, the mesh becomes tighter around the thicker portion of the fish's body. The fish then senses that it can't fit through and tries to back out, but as it does so, the thin lines that form the mesh become wedged underneath the fish's gill flaps, so that it now cannot go forward or backward. It is secured and now is at the fishermen's mercy. A good gill net can capture entire schools of fish at once.

A more active kind of gill netting is to fish runaround nets. The idea here is to surround a school of fish with a gill net, and then frighten them into the webbing. Locating a tight school is the problem. One solution is to hunt at night in summer waters, watching for the electric-light trails made by fish schools as they pass through bioluminescent plankton. When a school is sighted and then encircled, the vessel roars at full throttle above the fish while flashing a searchlight back and forth above the surface, causing the fish to panic and become gilled.

An even more elaborate offshoot of the gill net is the trammel net. A trammel net is really three nets that lie flat against each other. The two outside walls have wide meshes, but between them is a rather loose, fine-

Fish entangle themselves in a trammel net by forming a pocket of the small meshed webbing between the two big meshed walls.

meshed net. When a fish swims through the large outer meshes, it pushes against the looser, interior net so that a pocket is formed around the fish, which is then entombed. It is important that the two outer walls fit symmetrically together. Because a trammel net presents such a dense wall to fish, they don't usually swim into it on their own and instead must somehow be frightened into it.

A worldwide problem with gill nets is that they can become lost because of currents, storms, or negligence. In bygone days, the wayward fiber nets eventually rotted, but today's nylon nets keep catching and killing fish to no one's benefit as "ghost" nets.

GILL NETTING UNDER THE ICE

The physics are challenging

Because a gill net is like a long, vertical curtain of mesh, this simple gear is easily set, usually by boat, in liquid water. Although gill nets also fish well in winter, the problem with setting them stretched out under the ice is obvious. Innovative solutions exist, however.

A necessary step to fishing a gill net under the ice is to extend a rope down one hole made through the ice and out another, and then tie the net to the rope and pull it between the holes. The trick is in getting the rope passed through the holes. The simplest way is to make numerous holes in a line and to pass a rope from one hole to the next using a long, pliable stick. A marginal advance on this approach is the Murphy stick method, a less-than-auspicious name based on Murphy's Law—the idea that if something can go wrong, it will. A Murphy stick is a contraption consisting of an aluminum pipe with a pivot connecting to a longer length of pipe with a float and an eye on it. The fisherman passes the rope through the eye, and then passes the longer pipe section through the hole and aims it toward the next hole. When he spots its end there, he snatches the rope with a long hook.

The real advance in setting gill nets under the ice was via the ice jigger, an apparatus designed to walk a line under the ice. The ice jigger, invented around 1912 by a fisherman-blacksmith for use on Lake Manitoba in western Canada, consists mainly of a plank and two levers so arranged that a backward pull on an attached line translates into a forward thrust that pulls the plank along beneath the ice. When the jigger is placed under the ice, the buoyancy of the plank causes it float against the ice cover. A metal arm assumes a vertical position; a wooden arm in the slot of the plank remains horizontal. When the fisherman pulls the running line, the metal arm is pulled backward, the wooden arm is thrust upward, and a spike at its tip penetrates the ice, preventing backward movement of the jigger.

Using a jigger requires teamwork. A second operator has to try to follow the progress of the jigger by listening for the sound of the spike ticking against the undersurface of the ice in order to make a second hole to retrieve it. For night work, a mounted flashlight can provide a visible glow to the jigger. The beauty of this approach is that only two holes have to be made; this is no small advance in a region where ice could be six feet thick. So successful was this device that following its invention, it was soon being used across most of Canada.

H

HANDLINING

A truly tactile connection

Reduced to its most primitive form, spinning tackle might look like the old string and can rig. Wind line around a soda or beer container, tie a hook and sinker at the line's tag end, whirl it overhead, and let it fly, and the line follows just as it does off the most pricey open-face reel. Such a rig can conquer more than just panfish, too. Growing up near the shores of New York City, I often encountered Hispanic fishermen from the Caribbean who were experts with string and can. They'd put a hefty chunk of menhaden on their rig, fling it far distant, wedge the can between two boulders, place a stone on the line to secure it, and wait. Sooner or later the line would shoot out, and minutes after, a twelve-pound bluefish would be flopping on shore.

Swedish anglers use a slightly more sophisticated version. It's based on a wooden board that resembles a Ping-Pong paddle. An appropriate length of heavy braided line is wrapped around the paddle, with the weighted offering at the end. A deft flick of the wrist sends the rig into the surf, after which it is retrieved by hand.

Before the invention of wooden and bamboo surf rods, game fish were landed from beyond the breakers along the U.S. coasts with handlines. The typical gear consisted of a so-called "lead squid"—an oval-shaped lure, usually with a single large hook molded in and extending from its rear. Tin may have been alloyed with the lead to cause it not to sink too fast and to give it luster, although a rubdown with sand was necessary before each use to remove oxidation and regain shine. The lure often had a keel to help keep it swimming upright. The squid was tied to a cotton or linen line, perhaps twenty fathoms long, wrapped around a stick or coiled in a bucket.

The delivery and presentation were straightforward and crude. The line was held a few feet down from the squid, and the lure was swung overhead at high speed horizontally, or nearly so, and then released to fly seaward. When the lure splashed down, the line was hauled quickly, hand over hand, back to shore. Robert Barnwell Roosevelt, in *Superior Fishing* (1865), writes of the superiority in distance over rod and reel in the surf that could be achieved by casting a handline, but he says that the handline produced "far greater fatigue, and a painful over-exertion of the muscles of the arm that is almost unendurable to one who has not had steady practice." He also notes that the handline was "more killing probably than the rival method."

This tiring approach was best used when fish were sighted and the probability of hookups was high. In 1880, enormous schools of bluefish raided beaches in the mid-Atlantic. According to one camper at the Methodist Revivalist Campground at Ocean Grove, New Jersey, "No male was completely dressed that summer unless he had his line stuck in the rear pockets of his trousers, for one could never tell when there might be a run on." If the run happened on Sunday, he writes, it brought untold anguish, for no fishing was allowed that day.

HAND SPEARING

Never spear anything larger than you are

Throwing or jabbing a spear to land fish was done by almost every hunting culture, and it continues even in mechanized form in the western world. Today some who spear fish for sport go by this minimally protective rule: Never spear anything bigger than you are—unless you are certain to be able to get out of its way. But this doctrine is ignored by native fishermen who spear sharks for food in the surf near Acapulco, Mexico. Once a year, after the rainy season, a large freshwater lagoon breaks through a barrier island, spilling thousands of small fish into the ocean. Sharks arrive in great numbers but can be captured only in almost impossible circumstances. Waves there may be fifteen or twenty feet high. The fisherman looks for a shark's fin in an oncoming curl, and runs to where he guesses the shark will be after the wave breaks. Then he wades into the seething foam to try to sight the shark, which may be dozens of yards away or may brush his leg before he sees it. When he spots the shark, he forces his way through the suds to throw the spear, letting loops of line pay off as he runs to shore and the wounded fish thrashes toward the open sea. But if he lets out too much line or the next wave breaks too rapidly, the fish can't be held, and even a fifteen-foot shark may reappear almost instantly a hundred yards down the beach, still impaled but no longer tethered.

Natives of the Pacific's Gilbert and Ellice (now Tuvalu) Islands went hand spearing one better in their pursuit of tiger sharks. Perhaps to prove his manliness, when a native encountered a lone tiger shark, he would use himself as an attractant. When the shark charged, he'd slide to one side and use a knife to slit open its belly, with the fish's momentum causing the damage. He may have been tempted to shout the South Pacific version of "Olé!"

Palauans have a particularly rich spearfishing heritage. Among their most impressive applications is to hunt mullet and other small fish using throwing spears in only half a foot of water on reef flats. Considerable skill is needed to nail such diminutive targets, but hunting in groups makes the odds more favorable. When a school of mullet is spotted, the finder calls the other spearers, and each picks out a fish as the school panics and disperses. The fish are forced inland but have a natural inclination to reach deeper water, the net effect being that the chase runs parallel to the shore. A mullet tires as it jumps, so the fisherman counts the leaps as he chases.

After the fish's seventh jump, he throws a multipronged *taod* spear while on the run from about ten feet away. He uses a low, flat trajectory, aiming just in front of the fish.

Palauans hunt rays like trackers hunt rabbits in the snow. Rays make depressions in the bottom when foraging. Fishermen can identify the rays to species by the depressions they leave, some rounded, some triangular, some deeper than others. Because some kinds of sediment hold these forms crisply much longer than other kinds, a fisherman searching an area can gain a sense of how old the depression is and whether the fish is still likely in the vicinity by examining the ray's outline and the bottom type.

Palauans often use an unusual underwater spearfishing technique. Instead of cruising and searching, they dive to the bottom and lie flat and still, holding on to a coral head to stay down. Certain desirable species approach within range out of curiosity. These spearfishermen have other tricks in their arsenal as well. If a struggling jack or surgeonfish is left on the spear, other members of its school may crowd around it, offering easy targets for other spears. Rudderfish will lose their wariness and feed on algal fragments from a comrade's stomach a spear has pierced. Some jacks may be attracted to the fisherman if he makes glottal grunting sounds like those the fish make by grinding their pharyngeal teeth. Blowing bubbles from pursed lips also draws jacks.

The indigenous Ainu people of Japan's northernmost island, Hokkaido, have a long tradition of spearing king salmon from rivers on their spawning runs. But the Ainu spear differs from most in that it has a detachable hook. The hook rests in a groove in the spear and is attached to a rope that passes through a hole at the base of the groove. When a wading fisherman pierces any part of a salmon, the hook disengages and turns around in the fish's flesh, so that even less-than-solid strikes result in the salmon being landed. To aid in reaching salmon in their spawning rivers, the Ainu fishermen build clever weirs of stones that steer upstream-running fish toward locations where they are more easily hooked. Some of these weirs are so effective that the fish become trapped and can be landed with the old bear paw technique, swiping them up onto the bank.

Hand spearing often has been practiced under the cover of darkness, when fish may be less wary and may be momentarily confused by or attracted to a light. Nigerians spear Nile perch and other large fish at night using torches, flares, and carbide lamps. Back when sheepshead, large porgylike fish, were still found in New York waters, anglers speared them by torchlight in Long Island's bays. Vermonters continue to spear pike at night in early spring as they move into weedy shallows to spawn. Culverts are strategic stakeouts, especially at night, when lanterns allow practiced eyes to spot the dark shadow of an amorous pike and then to jab a five-tined fork at it.

Palauans also spear fish at night, particularly species such as parrotfish, surgeonfish, and wrasses, which are inactive in darkness. They've learned that if they shine a light into the eyes of a shark and then move it smoothly away, the shark will often follow the beam. Some Palauans find it comical to steer sharks directly into their fellow divers. But they do recognize limits to this behavior. One diver said, "You only do this to a friend—as a joke. A stranger would get very angry."

The skill attained by some practitioners in throwing spears at fish is incredible. Negley Farson in *Going Fishing* (1942) describes a Siwash Indian salmon fishery. The men speared the salmon and threw the ten- to fifteen-pound fish to their wives, who split them open, jerked out their insides, and threw the innards over their shoulders up the bank, where they rotted by the thousands. Farson found the stench appalling. But despite this unpleasantness, he was mesmerized by the spear throwing. The Siwash threw the two-pronged spears in the way the ancient Greeks threw the javelin—propelled from fingers placed against the butt. This meant that the projectile traveled in a parabola, falling into the fish. Yet despite the refraction of the light on the water and the movement of the fish, they rarely missed.

Farson thought that their approach was unnecessarily complicated, so he seized a spear by its midsection, compensated mentally for the refraction, and drove both barbs deep into a salmon. But the Siwash smiled and politely showed how his strong-armed method had merely succeeded in ruining a salmon for smoking: He'd broken its back and ruined a great deal of meat by driving the spear halfway through it.

HARPOONING GIANT FISH

Never look at a swordfish's eye

Spearing and harpooning may seem synonymous, and either way, the target feels a barb. But with spearing, the point normally remains attached to the shaft; with harpooning, the barb disengages from the shaft but remains connected to the fisherman with a long rope. Harpooning is for big game that can't easily be restrained: swordfish, tuna, and Moby Dick.

Harpooning has come a long way since the 1800s. Indeed, it became so effective that it contributed to the near commercial extinctions of bluefin tuna and swordfish over much of the high seas. In the nineteenth century, a swordfish harpoon consisted of a hardwood pole of about fifteen or sixteen feet in length, the bark left on to afford the harpooner a firmer grip. At one end was fitted an iron shank of about two feet long, upon which sat the working end of the harpoon, known variously as the "swordfish iron," "lily-iron," or "Indian-dart." This head toggled so that when a fish was struck, the harpooner could pull away the pole and the line would run straight to the iron at a right angle, thereby avoiding a straight upward force, which would tend to pull the iron out.

Swordfish in those times were harpooned from the bowsprits of sailing vessels, the harpooner getting set in a brace called a rest or pulpit. Not only were professional harpooning boats outfitted this way, but so were many mackerel schooners or packets, in order to capitalize on the occasional sighting of swordfish or tuna. Swordfish never come to the surface except in moderate, calm weather. Vessels cruising in search of them wandered on the fishing grounds, their crews never hesitating to hail other boats to ask if any swordfish had been seen. If so, they set course for where the fish were last noticed. A keen-eyed man was always stationed at the masthead;

experienced spotters could sight a tell-tale dorsal fin at a distance of two or three miles. When a fish was seen, the watch would sing out, and the vessel was aimed toward it.

The skipper, armed with a harpoon, would then take the pulpit and direct the man at the wheel by voice and gesture how to steer. Perhaps because of differences in the vibrations they generate, large sailing vessels had no difficulty in approaching swordfish, but small boats could not get near them. When the fish was from six to ten feet in front of the vessel, the harpooner struck it, not with a toss, but with a punch, just below the high portion of the dorsal fin. Then the pole was withdrawn and the line allowed to pull out as far as the fish would carry it, before the connection was passed to two men in a small boat.

In the 1800s, fishermen needed to quietly approach surfacing swordfish before throwing the harpoon; this still is true today despite improved equipment.

They would haul the wounded fish alongside, where they finished it with a whale-lance or whale-spade thrust into its gills.

But swordfish are especially pugnacious and sometimes sought revenge, an act noted far earlier in history. Pliny, the Roman naturalist, wrote that swordfish "hath a beake or bill sharply pointed, wherewith he will drive through the side and plankes of a ship, and gouge them so, that they shall sink withall." There are many accounts of wounded swordfish attacking vessels in the heyday of the U.S. fishery, as many as twenty times in one season for a single boat. In 1828, a ship was found with the stump of a swordfish blade protruding from its hull. The blade was driven through the external copper sheathing, an inch-thick wooden undersheathing, a three-inch-thick plank of hardwood, a one-foot-thick solid white oak timber, and a two-and-a-half-inch hard oak ceiling, finally penetrating an oil cask, where it stuck, not allowing a drop of oil to leak out. Another swordfish plunged its bill through an oak hull and two inches into a crewman's heel.

Harpooning during the recent past and present is not all that different from earlier practices, except that today's harpooners enjoy a few new advantages but far fewer fish. Off the Canadian Maritimes and New England, swordfish and bluefin tuna have been harpooned commercially from the bowsprits of modest-size power vessels. Calm seas are a necessity because this is a visual hunt, but the odds of finding fish are considerably greater with help from spotter planes. Often "stick boats" work as a team with a pilot in a small aircraft, who can scout the broad ocean far more efficiently for surfacing targets than can a boat crew, whose eyes are not that far above sea level.

Regardless of how the fish are spotted, the crew must carefully approach them or they will spook and dive. Electronic equipment is shut off as the boat, relatively narrow for its length and devoid of noisy spray rails, idles closer. The extended bowsprit, perhaps twenty feet in length, allows the harpooner to get well in front of the hull and within range of the fish. All harpoons for this kind of fishing have cables or ropes attached for fighting the prey or retrieving it should a dead fish sink. Some harpoons are electrified with insulated cable to provide a killing jolt.

The harpooner sits in front of the bowsprit, waiting for the right moment, as the captain keeps a steady speed (changing speed spooks the fish instantly) and closes the gap. With tuna, as a wary school pushes along, it may create a flow of water over itself that disrupts the sea surface, forming a wave called a "bauble." When near enough, the harpooner throws the spear, leading the target and either striking or missing. Sometimes a novice harpooner freezes when approaching his first swordfish, being transfixed by its eye. One who held his fire said that although his father had told him never to look at the eye, "that fish rolled his eye out and he fixed you, and you ain't the first. Nobody believes how big that eye is, and by the time they get over the surprise, the bow is past him and that fish is gone."

HAUL SEINING

Tricky maneuvering

Haul seining refers to fishing great seine nets off beaches, the "haul" being the difficult part. The concept is straightforward and not particularly clever: A seine is an arcing net with an upper float, or "cork," line and a lower weighted, or "lead," line that forms a vertical wall and herds fish back to the beach, with most being retained in a bag, or "cod end." But it's the tricks developed to implement these seining operations on a grand scale and in harsh environments that gained my respect as I watched them performed many times.

Haul seining was done on the sandbars at the mouth of the Co-lumbia River in Oregon, using horses to retrieve the heavy nets, and on North Carolina's Outer Banks for striped bass, where fishermen simply backed trucks over the wide beach to haul the fish in. Chinook Indians would haul seine with five-hundred-foot nets, bringing the fish near shore and then subduing them with clubs. Haul seining also is practiced in the Caspian Sea for sturgeon and other species with nets a kilometer long and twelve meters deep, and where the fishing grounds were prepared using a steamboat trailing a kind of plow. But nowhere did it reach the level of refinement than on the beaches of the Hamptons in eastern Long Island, New York.

During spring and fall, huge schools of striped bass move along the Hamptons' ocean shore, together at times with bluefish, weakfish, American shad, and a host of other species. To land these fish, haul-seining "baymen" rode the beaches in their trucks, lugging dories on trailers, looking for signs of the schools, such as splashes and bird aggregations. Then, if sea conditions allowed, they got to work. In earlier times, the crew manned oars. In later years, several crewmen jumped into the sixteen-foot-long dory and started up an outboard motor, which was mounted in an internal engine well for protection from the waves. With the trailer positioned, the crew chief watched the breaking waves, and when he thought it was exactly the right moment, he barked an order to the truck driver. The driver then gunned the truck in reverse right into

Launching the dory for haul seining in the surf, East Hampton, New York.

the shallows, and then braked suddenly, which caused the dory to shoot off its rollers into the surf. The truck driver next tried to accelerate the vehicle out of danger; if it became stuck, a second truck it had been tied to towed it to higher ground.

Meanwhile, with the outboard motor already running, the vessel quickly made it past the breakers out onto the more quiescent rollers. The crew then fed as much as three thousand feet of net, which measured twenty-five to forty feet from top to bottom, out in an arc, so that the net terminated a little before the dory reached the surf zone, hundreds of feet away from its starting point. Here the dory operator revved the outboard, traveling on the back of a wave to be winched onto the repositioned waiting trailer, and the dory and its crew were plucked from the sea. But even this was not straightforward: If the vessel lost headway, it would wallow in a trough, where it could flip; if the dory rode too far forward and picked up speed, it could plunge down the face of the wave as it

Landing a haul seine with a large catch, East Hampton, New York.

was breaking, jamming its bow in the sand and pitchpoling into a fast and possibly deadly somersault.

The next problem was to retrieve the heavy, massive net and its potentially weighty contents. This was harder than it might seem. Each end of the net was attached to a pickup truck, but East Hampton beaches are narrower than those in the Outer Banks, and simply backing up the trucks far landward was not an option. Electric winches could not handle the great strain either. The baymen solved this problem by mounting homemade winches that ran directly off the drive shafts of the truck engines when kept in neutral. They ran a "whipping line," a hank tied to the nearest reachable part of the submerged net, to the winches. By constantly repeating the process as the net inched closer, they could draw it to the beach. But even this mundane task required a certain artistry. Because the strong waves and typical sideways longshore current pulled the entire net downstream, the two truck operators needed to keep adjusting their positions in regard to not only the closing net, but also to the net's longitudinal position along the beach.

With the net set correctly in place, any fish in its interior half circle were trapped, unless they leaped over the float line or the leadline lifted. As the net drew nearer, some fish became gilled in the mesh, but the bulk remained herded in its pocket. Smaller catches could simply be dragged onto shore, but sometimes the hauls were enormous and needed to be bailed from the sea until reduced enough to be beached. As equipment was improved, sets that produced four-hundred- and five-hundred-box hauls occasionally occurred, at about one hundred pounds of fish to the box.

Unfortunately, this colorful fishery is already on its deathbed. Because the East Hampton beaches are also populated by many surf casters, an ongoing "surf and turf" feud developed between the two factions. The anglers did not appreciate that the baymen set their nets around schools of game fish the casters had located, or that the baymen often picked out the part of the catch they intended to keep and allowed the remaining "trash" fish to die on the sands. But the baymen operated with the confidence that they had ruled the beaches for generations before the surf casters had appeared, and felt that they didn't need to change their ways. After much political wrangling, commercial haul seining was banned. It now survives only in subsidized form, with one crew performing a yearly autumn survey with a shortened net for the New York State Department of Environmental Conservation, only sixty hauls per year from extinction.

HEAVING TUNA

Over-the-top fishing

The various tunas of the world's oceans are among the most sought-after food and game fish. Sleek, streamlined torpedoes, they never stop swimming as they power through the seas to nourish a unique metabolism—one that results in a kind of warm-bloodedness that is rare among fish.

But although tunas are often most easily secured on hook and line, commercial fishermen don't have time to spend fighting the long, glamorous battles with tuna that anglers seek. To quickly subdue and land tuna in commercial quantities, a "heaving" technique was developed to get them out of the water almost as soon as they are hooked, before they can turn their bodies and turn on their might. To do this, it helps to have the fishermen situated close to sea level. This is accomplished by chaining temporary metal walkways with railings off the vessel's sides.

For heaving to work, the tuna school must be whipped into a feeding frenzy. But first they have to be located. Before the advent of sophisticated electronics to detect submerged schools, fishermen such as those from the Atlantic island of Madeira trolled wooden lures from rudimentary outriggers. When a bigeye tuna struck, the crew tried to hold its schoolmates by chumming with crippled mackerel and by turning on high-pressure hoses and spraying the sea surface to simulate panicked baitfish. When the tuna responded, the fishermen deployed live mackerel on a stout hook, fished off a pole with heavy line tied to about ten feet of a light line. When the tuna struck, the light line broke, stopping the tuna's attempt to turn and dive. The fish then was brought to the side of the boat and lifted, or gaffed if too large.

Indonesian fishermen used a primitive version of heaving tuna. Several fishermen ventured many miles out to sea in a single large, open boat armed with bamboo poles and barbless hooks. Setting out at dawn, they used a net and homemade goggles to capture hundreds of baitfish, which they kept alive by flooding the boat's bottom. They later used these fish as chum. When a school of predatory skipjack tuna erupted at the surface, the men went into action, expertly hooking fish after fish with a single fluid motion of the pole that landed each fish in the boat. The long day ended after sunset, when the crew navigated by the stars.

Albacore fishermen in Australia, South Africa, and elsewhere also jigged in feeding frenzies. This species was generally smaller in size, so the fishermen simply used the momentum of the strikes along with brute force to heave the fish over their heads into the center of the vessel. In some locations, the lines from more than one pole were entwined so that teams of fishermen could heave together. If a giant bluefin elbowed in, however, it was the fishermen who got heaved.

HIT-AND-RELEASE

A rarefied sport

A very small number of people practice the seemingly perverse sport of "hit-and-release," or hookless fly fishing. But this idea should not be too easily dismissed—these rebels may simply be well ahead of their time. A hookless fly is nothing more than a conventional fly with its hook cut off at the bend. This arrangement still allows the angler to experience the real challenge in trout fishing: getting the fish to rise and take the fly. Peter Bodo, in a November 7, 1999, *New York Times* column, writes of his introduction to the sport: "Eliminate the hook, and you eradicate any possibility of hooking and fighting the fish. We were either taking catch-and-release fly-fishing to the next level—or reducing it to its most absurd conclusion."

In *Northern Waters* (1999), Jan Zita Grover describes Minnehaha Creek in Minneapolis as her Zen fishing paradise; Zen because its urban but nonetheless lovely and wooded waters were beguiling but virtually fishless. This didn't stop her from making it her home river, and she fished there often. But in recognition of its missing piscine element, she conducted her fly casting with a piece of yarn rather than an actual fly. For her, the absence of fish was nicely balanced by the familiarity with the creek the short trip to it allowed, being able to watch a variety of insect hatches, and the dearth of other fishermen.

Another practitioner of hookless fishing who fished in a stream with actual trout said that if you don't respond to the take, the trout won't spit the fly out and you will be able to play with it for a while, and that the oneness with nature achieved by this approach is well worth the catches forsaken. Will this rather subtle approach catch on? Bodo points out that catch-and-release was once considered a big fat joke too.

HOMEMADE LURES

It's not always necessity that gives birth to invention

Angling can be a highly creative endeavor. Sometimes inspiration for new lures takes weird forms, often from familiar objects that become mutated in basement and garage workshops. A Cape Cod acquaintance of mine swears by a homemade bluefish lure crafted from silverware knives. With a hole punched in the knife tip and the hook fastened to the handle end, it casts like a bullet and swims with the darting motion and flash of an anchovy or similar baitfish. Another surf caster capitalized on the rapaciousness of bluefish to land them on a variety of comical lures, including ones made from Barbie and Ken dolls fished backward so that when a bluefish struck, the torso was engulfed, sharklike, by the bluefish. This twisted fisherman also cast a lure created from a sex vibrator, which he called a "pink plump popper." Sealed to become waterproof, armed with hooks, and fished while turned on, it supposedly outperformed some traditional lures.

Of course, getting bluefish to strike is often not a challenge. One fellow demonstrated their rapaciousness by tying a flip-flop to fifty-pound-test line and dragging it across the surface over a school of feeding blues. They chewed it to pieces.

HOOKLESS ANGLING

Who needs barbs?

Gar are fearsome-looking freshwater predators that belong to an ancient branch of fishes. Looking a bit like a slimmed-down pike with an extended muzzle, they rush minnows and other prey, often grabbing them lengthwise in their dentally overendowed jaws. Several gar species are distributed across much of eastern North America, with one, the alligator gar, reaching more than two hundred pounds. Because gar have such extraordinary teeth but such narrow snouts, it's hard to hold them using traditional hooks. However, anglers have found a remarkably effective alternative: hookless lures.

The secret is to exchange the idea of penetrating the jaws for the notion of simply snagging the teeth. Nylon does the job exceedingly well. Commercial lures incorporating it are available, such as the Gar Getter, which is made from an eight-inch shot of fine nylon strands and a split ring, held together by a plastic zip tie. Do-it-yourselfers take a length of soft braided nylon rope, melt one end with a lighter, and then unravel the other, leaving about one and a half inches for the head.

Because there are no hooks on these lures, it's important to curb the tendency to strike; instead, you let the fish run with the offering to allow time for it to chew on the nylon. A caught gar will tangle the fibers, but the lure can be combed straight. Partly because of this innovation, gar fishing is growing more popular, and one Missourian is even attempting to build a gar resort.

Other thin-snouted fish that have been taken on hookless lures include the billfish. Marlin and sailfish can be taken by trolling an artificial "hairy" bait, which becomes entangled on the rough surfaces of their extended snouts. And needlefish are caught in the Black Sea on tassels of nylon thread.

In the San Francisco Bay area, striped bass can be caught while fishing with whole staghorn sculpin, known locally as bullhead. These sculpin, like the rest of the genus, have spines that extend backward on the top of the head. Stripers swallow them (and almost all other fish too) headfirst so that their spines don't become stuck in their throats. Some anglers clip off the bullhead's spines, believing that they become friendlier to bass. But show-off fishermen who have caught enough stripers have been known to simply tie the sculpin on as bait without a hook, landing bass with nothing but the hold the spines provide.

Perhaps the ultimate in hookless angling is conducted in the Amazon for whale catfish of the family Cetopsidae, voracious predators similar to piranhas in their ability to devour a victim rapidly. Whale catfish have large, round bodies and can easily burrow into torn flesh by biting and rotating, almost like a drill. Because they cling so tenaciously, they can be caught by soaking a hunk of meat in the river for a while and then retrieving it. One expert recommended a bait that goes well beyond the lowly earthworm: the head of an ox.

HUXING PIKE

Not for animal-rights activists

William Radcliffe, in *Fishing from the Earliest Times* (1921), quotes a T. Barker on the old-time practice of live-baiting pike with the aid of waterfowl, known as huxing: "The principal sport to take a Pike is to take a Goose or Gander or Duck, take one of the Pike Lines as I have showed you before; tye the line under the left wing and over the right wing, and about the bodie as a man weareth his belt; turne the Goose off into a pond where the pikes are; there is no doubt of sport with much pleasure betwixt the Goose and the Pike. It is the greatest pleasure that a noble Gentleman in Shropshire doth give his friends for entertainment. There is no question among all this fishing but we shall take a brace of good Pikes."

In huxing, a baited hook was attached to the leg or wing of a duck or goose, at a length to dangle about midwater, before driving the bird into the water. Two other accounts are interesting for their language and imagery. A John Donton, traveling in Ireland around 1690, describes it: "Thus they throw the fishing-goose into the water, who sports and preens herself with seeming pleasure enough, until some unmannerly fish seizes the baited hook and interrupts her diversion by giving her a tug which douces her almost under water, this commonly frightens her so as to put her to the wing, but if the fish be heavy she is forced to float upon the water, and though in romance the knight generally slays the giant, yet if the pike be of the larger sort Mrs Goose without the assistance of the spectators is sometimes like to go down to the pike instead of the pike coming up to her."

Huxing appears to have been dying out by the turn of the nineteenth century. In *Rural Sports* (1802), the Reverend William Daniel describes it as practiced in Scotland: "'Upon the Islands a number of *Geese* were collected by the Farmers, who occupied the surrounding banks of the *loch*, after baited lines of two or three feet long had been tied to the *legs* of their geese, they were driven into the water; steering naturally homewards, in different directions, the baits were soon swallowed; a violent and often tedious struggle ensued, in which, however, the *geese* at length prevailed, though they were frequently much exhausted before they reached the shore.' This method has not been so long relinquished, but there are old persons upon the spot, who were active promoters of the amusement."

Times have changed, and anyone huxing today surely would be arrested for cruelty to animals.

ICE SPEARING WITH FISH DECOYS

Preternatural patience required

The ice spearer personifies patience. Sitting in a shanty, the practitioner stares down into the depths through a large hole, waiting—always at the ready—to throw a spear at a sturgeon or pike that may suddenly glide into view. But an all-day session may present no targets, and even if a fish does materialize, the thrust may miss the intended victim. Going fishless under these circumstances is no embarrassment.

Ice spearing occurs only where there is seasonal ice, and lots of it. This means a band across the far northern United States and Canada, where frozen water lasts long enough during winter to support and warrant the placement of shanties that may be left in place for weeks or months—until the ice begins to weaken as spring approaches. Ice spearing is most frequently, and perhaps most passionately, conducted in Minnesota and Wisconsin.

Lake sturgeon, behemoths that can reach eight feet in length, are the big game of winter spearing. Michigan has a sturgeon-spearing tradition, but the numbers of sturgeon are so low there that the state's 2001 season was conducted on just one lake, and it was closed after thirty-five minutes, when the quota of five sturgeon was reached.

Winter spearing of lake sturgeon is almost a religion on Wisconsin's sprawling but shallow Lake Winnebago, where fishermen hope to impale specimens that can reach eight feet in length. Not only does the shanty provide shelter from the cold, but its darkened interior allows the fisherman to see clearly through water that is illuminated to some degree from light passing through the surrounding ice. Native Americans, who invented ice spearing, did not use shanties, but instead used spearing tents. One type was seven feet tall and allowed the fisherman to sit down with a long-handled spear extending outside the tent. A second, more portable style covered about two-thirds of the fisherman's prone body. Balsam branches provided some measure of comfort as flooring.

A contemporary sturgeon spear is about six feet long, with multiple barbed tines. Because it would be difficult to hold for hours, it usually is hung directly above the hole in the shanty on a headless nail. Fishermen's success rates vary tremendously by year in Lake Winnebago, dependent on water clarity. During winters with light snow cover, the sun's rays penetrate the ice, producing algae blooms that greatly reduce the visibility of sturgeon. In the old days, some fishermen tried to compensate by placing eggshells on the lake bottom to provide a light-colored backdrop; with new rules requiring that everything put in the water is later removed, fishermen now use white PVC tubes instead.

The odds of encountering a sturgeon target are poor when simply gazing at a randomly made hole. To increase the chances of seeing a sturgeon, fishermen capitalize on the fish's curiosity by dangling weighted fish decoys beneath their holes, often six-inch to one-foot-long homemade facsimiles of local species or imagined ones. Some are gaudily colored, others drab. Many have sheet-metal fins. Not only fish are simulated; some decoys represent frogs, turtles, birds, or small mammals. These attractors are recognized as folk art and are avidly collected, with those from "name" makers sometimes commanding extraordinary prices. Indeed, just as with bird decoys, there is a whole world of fish decoy carvers whose work never gets wet.

Ice fishing, including spearing, invokes strong reactions; people seem to either love it or hate it. The most smitten sometimes take risks to practice their sport. I'm one of those, and I have fished on ice so thin that it slowly bowed as I sat on my stool, with water beginning to flow up through the hole. In Lake Ontario, it is known that in certain bays there are concentrations of walleye under early, thin ice. To catch them, some anglers creep on boards placed over the barely frozen surface. Occasionally on large lakes or rivers, a huge portion of ice breaks off, carrying dozens of anglers with it, their rescue sometimes dependent on helicopters.

Some recommend that as soon as a speared sturgeon is landed, it should be thrown upon the ice outside the shanty and allowed to freeze to keep the meat sweeter and fresher. But getting the fish out of the hole is not always easy—a big sturgeon is a formidable adversary, even with a spear in its back. In *A Place on the Water* (1993), Jerry Dennis wrote of a Michigan ice fisherman who saw a nearby shanty suddenly begin shaking. One wall fell outward and crashed onto the ice, then another, then the third and fourth walls fell and the roof collapsed, leaving a man standing in the open, struggling to get a six-foot-long sturgeon away from the hole while hugging the fish.

J

JUBILEES AND NUMBS

Fish don't get more cooperative

There are a few places in the world where fish become grounded often enough that they form fisheries of opportunity, usually picking up nicknames and achieving at least locally legendary status. After all, what could be easier than simply bending over to make a catch?

Technically, "jubilees" occur under very particular conditions along a specific area of the Gulf of Mexico coastline, but the term may refer to any sudden hand-gathering fish bonanza. During summer, when residents of the eastern shore of Mobile Bay, Alabama, notice a continuing gentle east wind together with a rising tide following a previous overcast day, they go down to the shore, buckets in hand, expecting a jubilee. If the situation develops, fish and crabs begin to leap and crawl on shore, and the immediate shallows are filled with life. Locals cry, "Jubilee!" And word spreads, with people running to the shore. Jubilees, known since at least 1860, are so ingrained in the local culture that someone published a 750-recipe cookbook for preparing the harvest, titled *Recipe Jubilee.*

The festive nature of this easy harvest is balanced by the distress felt by the animals. Jubilees bring fish and crabs to the beach because the east wind blows oxygenated surface waters away from shore, which are replaced by low-oxygen bottom waters. This surge of uninhabitable water drives organisms ahead of it, pinning them between two environments, land and sea, neither of which can sustain them.

I once saw a highly localized jubilee in Hempstead Harbor in western Long Island Sound, not far from New York City. In this embayment, September's east winds sometimes drive surface water to the opposite shore, tilting deoxygenated bottom water back in replacement, just as happens in Mobile Bay. When I arrived, a few adults were harvesting crabs and young lobsters, and children were collecting pipefish for aquariums. When I waded in, the shallows were filled with a ribbon of life. Bottom fish were everywhere, especially juvenile flounder, which were so crowded together that they resembled the interlocking fish in an Escher drawing. Fortunately, in this case the wind abated, and most of the afflicted organisms appeared to survive.

Another climatically based hand-gathering fishery is the "numbs" of North Carolina—cold snaps that yield sea trout. *American Fishes* (1888), by G. Brown Goode, includes a letter from an observer from Onslow County, North Carolina, who writes: "When we have extremely cold and cloudy weather, and I believe also windy weather for three or four days, the Trout at the mouth of New River are benumbed, and on the first sunny day rise to the surface, and after a day or two die and sink to the bottom or are washed ashore. As soon as they rise, there are generally hundreds of men ready with nets, dip nets, gigs, and in some instances, nothing but their hands and boats, to pick them up. They are sometimes washed ashore in long heaps, two and three feet deep, for a considerable distance. When these 'numbs' occur, it is generally known through this and the adjoining counties, and carts and wagons come for the fish by hundreds—sometimes from a distance of fifty or sixty miles." The observer reports numbs during the winters of 1877 and 1879, but says they do not occur frequently.

JUDAS FISH

Piscine accomplices

Oppian notes in *Halieutica* that the passionate desire of the normally wary mullet when about to spawn "renders it so unguarded" that if a male or female is caught, fastened to a line, allowed to swim to sea, and then gently drawn back to land, shoals of the opposite sex will follow the captive close to shore and into waiting nets. This "Judas fish" technique worked well in those ancient times, and it still works well in modern Greece.

If a single Judas fish is effective, imagine a Judas school of fish. The ancient Greek Aelian writes of a place called Athena's Isle, which contained a lagoon where schools of tame mackerel were fed. Fishermen threw food to them but observed a "treaty of peace," so the fish were immune from pursuit and attained a great age. After being fed, they were thought to repay the fishermen by leaving the harbor to meet "strange" mackerel. The strange mackerel did not flee from their brethren, and the tame mackerel encircled them and held them in place until the fishermen could net them. Meanwhile, the tame fish were said to return hastily to the lagoon to await their afternoon meal. Although such extreme cooperation appears apocryphal, Aelian concludes his account: "And this happens every day."

JUGGING

Following the fleet

Jugging is associated with catfish, lazy southern U.S. rivers, and boys leading a Huck Finn existence. In this simple approach, baits are hung on lines under jugs. As most often practiced, large sets of these rigs are followed by boat in the slow currents of big rivers. The jugs should only be buoyant enough to suspend the rig, because large containers catch the breeze and drift too fast; quart-size jugs are sometimes recommended. Glass jugs are avoided, because they can break if the fish runs them against the side of the boat. To follow the floats at night, reflector tape may be applied to the jugs.

Baits are hung to ride about two feet off the bottom. The fisherman uses a net to scoop up a lively "fish-on" jug, grabs the line, and hauls in the fish. But big catfish often tow jugs a long distance, requiring a chase. Catfish eat nearly anything organic, and almost everything has been used for bait while jugging. Nineteenth-century commercial juggers on the Ohio River who sought giant flathead catfish supposedly used baseball-size chunks of beef, small chickens, and even live kittens.

Although the principles remain the same, jugging has evolved in different ways elsewhere. In *Somewhere down the Crazy River* (1992), authors Paul Boote and Jeremy Wade describe how on the Congo, a *mbomi mbisi* (literally, "fish murderer") may use an elegantly uncomplicated drift rig to catch the goliath tigerfish, an awesome predator with teeth that rival those of barracuda. A five- or ten-liter jerry can floats a line leading to a two- to three-kilogram boulder. (The boulder's weight is carefully selected; too light and the hook may not set, too heavy and the hook may tear out the fish's mouth.) Not far below the buoy is attached a heavy wire connected to a large single hook, which is baited with a scaly fish of appropriate size. As the rig works slowly downstream, the fish bait spins in the flow a meter below the surface.

The "fish murderer" follows several such rigs in his pirogue as they drift down the river. When a goliath strikes, certain characteristics of the arrangement serve to subdue the great fish. The line is set to be more than 20 percent longer than the depth of the water, allowing the goliath slack to head for the surface with its tendency to jump, but this lifts the boulder, the resistance further setting the hook. If the fish dives, it fights the pull of the float.

Once hooked, the landing of a goliath tigerfish is not so easy. The fisherman must grab the line below the float, harpoon at the ready, and after spearing his catch, tip the pirogue sideways to land the fish, and then quickly bail the excess water.

The British use a jugging approach to catch the European sea bass, a close relative of the American striped bass, almost a "striper" without stripes. Sea bass often inhabit sharp riptides, which can become mountainous when the wind blows against the flow. One way of catching sea bass in these locations without risking capsizing is to drop baited *dhans*—bamboo canes weighted at one end beneath foam flotation, with a flag on top—at the uptide ends of large rips. A fast boat can place twenty or so *dhans* and race around the outside of a shallow rip (often over a reef) to pick up the buoys and their catches. Larger boats may work in pairs, fishing about one hundred *dhans* at once.

K

KITE FISHING

Sometimes wind is a good thing

Employing a kite to catch fish seems almost whimsical, but it has a surprisingly rich sportfishing history and can be highly effective for enticing even the most challenging game fish. Simple versions of wind-aided fishing are practiced worldwide wherever open water, fish, and a breeze can be found. In England, anglers on piers sometimes float baits on sheets of newspaper to present them farther out on windy days. In Malta, fishermen seeking garfish made little rafts of cork and reeds, using a small sail to catch the wind and propel it offshore, and a tether to retrieve it. Underneath the raft hung numerous lines and baited hooks.

Modern big-game kite fishing was invented off Santa Catalina, California. One observer wrote that when he visited the island in 1900, the tuna were plentiful and could be taken by merely trolling a flying fish one hundred feet behind a launch. But when he returned in 1910, he found that it was impossible to persuade the now more educated tuna to take the bait unless it was skittered in front of their noses from a kite. Early applications there involved attaching a twenty-eight-inch silk kite with a rag tail (with wine corks added for flotation) to seven hundred feet of old fishing line. The fisherman's line was tied to the kite about twenty feet from the bait with a piece of cotton twine. When a fish struck, the twine would break and the kite would fall into the sea as the fight began. This technique resulted in some notable catches for the era, such as enormous tuna and swordfish to 463 pounds, with one leading the launch for fourteen hours and twenty-nine miles, and sounding forty-eight times.

Kite rigs have improved over time and are used from boat and shore, mostly in tropical and subtropical marine areas where steady breezes are prevalent and clear waters accentuate their effectiveness. Australians appear particularly enamored with kite fishing. They use a range of models that work in winds of as little as three knots to more than seventy knots. They also work well for shore anglers where there are strong riptides that would lift up and sweep away a conventionally tethered line. Some beach fishermen Down Under use longlines off kites with up to the legal limit of twenty-five hooks. A bottle filled with sand or water keeps such a rig low in the water column. The new generation of kites used in Australia also allows a tremendous reach of three thousand feet or more.

Kite fishing has evolved, like most things modern, into a high-speed version. Rather than passively let the wind carry the bait, today some tuna anglers pull kite rigs behind sportfishing boats. When feeding tuna are surfacing, they sometimes spook from engine noise or bow-wave pressure as the fishing boat attempts to troll near them. But by mounting a kite rig from the side of the vessel and then approaching at the correct angle, bait can be presented from hundreds of feet away, and the fish remain unalarmed. And by traveling at twenty knots or more, the flying fish or similar bait skips over the surface in twenty- to thirty-foot bounds, so exciting tuna that they have been known to leap four feet high to nail one.

KLONKING

Sounds good to catfish

Klonking is a European technique based on sound for attracting Old World catfish known as the giant wels. Wels and all other catfish possess superior sensitivity to sound because of unique internal morphology, in which special bones called Weberian ossicles connect the inner ear to the air bladder, a sound resonator. As a result, the hearing range of catfish may be as much as four times that of other fish.

Klonking is used mainly on large rivers such as the Seine in France and the Po in Italy, where the wels dwell. These big waters support big fish: Two-hundred-pounders are still caught, and scientists believe wels may have reached six hundred pounds in earlier times. There is an old saying in angling: "Big fish, big bait." Wels are known to prey on a very big bait—waterfowl. At least one fisherman on the River Seille in France subdues these behemoths with a big bait not to be used by the soft-hearted: a live duck, tethered near shore at night and bearing a large treble hook. Recently, a visiting sport angler fished for wels in the Romanian Danube for ten days without success, but then was taken under the wing of a native klonking expert. They rowed to a deep meandering stretch of the river and rigged a heavy handline, equipping it with a lead weight, a rusty hook, and half a dozen large leeches (elsewhere in Europe, large worms are used, two per point of the treble hook). This delightful offering was fished about four feet off the bottom as the boat drifted, with the line wound around the handle of a homemade wooden klonk. A klonk, also known in Europe as a *butschalo*, is shaped like the lower leg of a hoofed animal, the backside being concave. The fisherman held the line by the first two fingers of the hand gripping the klonk. Then, using the klonk like a paddle, he dipped the tool into the water and stroked quickly down and then up above the water surface, so that the concavity, which had trapped an air bubble, produced a loud *woomp* sound. After doing this about six times, the old expert jigged the bait to make the leeches wave enticingly. Not only was this technique weird, but it was effective. By the end of the day, after covering several miles of the Danube, the fishermen had caught many catfish.

Other sounds may also attract fish. A friend who fished the Amazon watched as his native guides beat the water to attract piranha. Fishery workers sometimes draw spawning muskellunge to net by making whomping sounds with a canoe paddle. Yellow perch may be attracted to motor vibrations; anglers sometimes increase their catches by leaving their engines idling while fishing. Perch may also be drawn to the vibrations of a gasoline-powered auger drilling through ice. One day on a North Dakota lake where no one was catching anything, a team of anglers put together a catch of perch with one fellow drilling holes and the other fishing along behind him.

KYLIE FISHING

Death comes whirling

Pity the unsuspecting mullet. A whirling pointed cross, known as a kylie, may be coming its way.

The word *kylie* was coined after an aboriginal word for "throwing stick," a tool used by Australian tribes. Their version was originally made of wood but later was replaced by metal, which penetrates the water more effectively. Some mullet hunters make their own kylies from hoop iron, flattening it with a hammer, drilling two holes into it, riveting it, and then smashing it with a hammer again. These deeper-water kylies are in a cross shape, with the throwing arm longer than the others. But all have V-cuts to create two cutting points. A V-shaped kylie is made for shallow water.

Kylie fishing is effective under the right conditions, which include bright sunshine and flat water. Polaroid sunglasses also help. The chief prey of the kylie fishermen are mullet, called "flatheads" Down Under. Kylie fishermen chase flatheads across the sand flats, throwing their whirling weapons when in range.

LA MATTANZA AND TONNARA

Fish can't solve mazes

Fish fences may be erected in wonderfully creative patterns to form difficult-to-escape-from labyrinths. The principle is that migrating fish encounter the barrier, turn and trace it, and are drawn by its design into one or more chambers that encourage entrance but discourage escape. In the United States, gear of this type is commonly known as a trap or pound net.

The most famous of labyrinths is the *tonnara* in the Mediterranean Sea for bluefin tuna. This fishery is conducted in May at Favignana, an island off Sicily. It is one of the last of many that existed for a thousand years or more around the perimeter of the sea. All were predicated on the placement of a deep underwater funnel net in the migratory path of the tuna, together with a series of chambers in which they could be sectioned off and corralled until harvested.

The second-century naturalist poet Oppian describes a Roman *tonnara* thus: "Dropped in the water are nets arranged like a city. There are rooms and gates and deep tunnels and atria and courtyards. The tuna arrive in great haste, drawn together like a phalanx of men who march in rank: there are the young, the old, the adults. And they swim, innumerable, inside the nets and the movement is

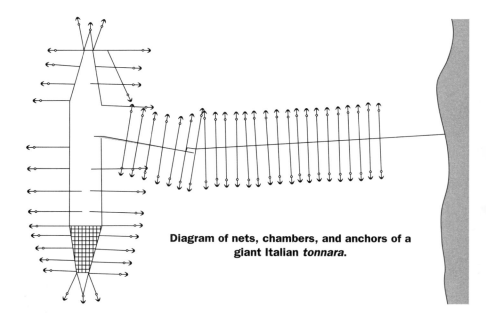

**Diagram of nets, chambers, and anchors of a
giant Italian *tonnara*.**

stopped only when . . . there is no more room for new arrivals; then the net is pulled up and a rich haul of excellent tuna is made." In the 1300s, *tonnara* were so important an industry in Sicily, and such a source of revenue for the king, that a law was passed declaring that *tonnara* workers, from the leader to the last shopboy, were immune from legal proceedings, civil or criminal, during the spring bluefin season.

Because of its enormous size, working a *tonnara* is no simple task. Almost four hundred anchors are needed to hold it in place, and these range from 660 to nearly 4,000 pounds. The final chamber alone is one hundred yards long, seventy-five feet wide, and hangs one hundred feet down. Three barrier nets that steer fish to the chambers are all more than fourteen hundred yards long. Today, with tuna smaller and fewer in number, crew sizes have shrunk. But in the past, workers known as *tonnarotti* numbered as many as one hundred, all needed for setting up the net at great depths, fishing, removal, and preparation and maintenance of the gear.

Large catches are possible; in 1986, the last good year before a decline, 2,551 tuna were landed at Favignana. But back in more bounteous times, Sicilian *tonnara* caught as many as three thousand bluefin in a single day.

The landing of the trapped tuna, known as *la mattanza*, or "the slaughter," became a tourist attraction. A couple hundred sightseers were towed out in a seventy-five-foot-long boat with no engine and left in a strategic position. Then, as the bottom net in the *camera della morte*, or "chamber of death," is slowly lifted, huge dark shapes were seen swirling below. When forced higher, they churned the surface into a white froth, soaking and

Tonnara **workers gaffing a giant bluefin tuna from the chamber of death.**

delighting the crowd. The fish were gaffed, one by one, by five teams of eight men and hauled into a boat in an ancient ritual that some viewers found both shocking and beautiful.

LEAF SWEEPS

Kind of a harvest wreath

This primitive fish-catching technique, once used throughout Oceania, worked despite its overwhelming lack of sophistication. A leaf sweep is a rope festooned with leaves used to herd and capture fish. Called *hukilau* in Hawaii and *ruul* in Palau, the device resembles a giant Christmas tree. It took the better part of a day for a dozen workers to construct several hundred yards of a leaf sweep by weaving palm fronds around a woody vine or rope. When completed, it was piled onto two bamboo rafts and transported onto a reef flat on a falling tide. The two rafts were pulled apart while paying the sweep into the water, with the rafts moving in opposing arcs to close a circle. When the enclosure was complete, the fishermen gathered the sweep into a smaller coil. When the corral was only a few meters wide, the crew leader would give the signal to begin spearing the herded fish, which were not forcibly concentrated but simply afraid to cross the unnatural barrier. A certain degree of stealth was necessary—too much commotion and the fish would stampede the sweep.

A more sophisticated version of the sweep is used in southeast Asia. Fishermen drive fish into nets that resemble giant dustpans by hauling a frightening line toward their mouths. This frightening line is nothing more than a better-made leaf sweep.

LOG FISHING

Fish in the trees

To natives of small Pacific islands, a floating log was a gift from afar. The wood served as material for building homes and canoes in a part of the world where suitable lumber often was in short supply. Black soil bound in its roots was rinsed with rainwater to remove sea salt, then used to enrich plots where papaya trees were planted. Igneous rocks mixed with the dirt were treasured for toolmaking in a region where the hardest natural objects were seashells and coral rock. But before a floating log was recovered, it often was mined for the fish assemblages that drifted along with it.

For reasons still unknown, many tropical pelagic fish gather, often in large schools, under logs and other floating objects. Even a single palm frond may be a temporary home for schools of dolphinfish, jacks, oceanic triggerfish, and skipjack tuna. Single logs have been observed to hold tuna schools of several thousand individuals. But not all of these fish magnets are created equally. Fishermen from Tobi and the Caroline Islands have found that the longer the log has been in the water, with a consequently greater amount of seaweed and gooseneck barnacles hanging from it, the more fish it attracts.

Log fishing in the southwestern Pacific is not a random act; because of climatological and oceanographic factors, log season begins in July and peaks between September and December. Trees first wash from riverbanks during rainy season in New Guinea and the Philippines, and then are carried to the islands by the appropriate, but seasonally shifting, currents.

Modern commercial tuna-fishing operations now mimic the islanders' approach. When a log is found to host tuna, a radio beacon is attached to it and its position monitored. The net is then set around the log near dawn or dusk so that the tuna are less likely to see it and to dive to avoid it.

LONG-DISTANCE CONVENTIONAL CASTING

Fancy footwork required

Sometimes the fish are just a bit too far off shore to reach without herculean casts. But anglers have long searched for edges in gear and techniques that add feet or yards to their tosses. And, as with almost all measurable human endeavors, casting became a competitive sport, which generated even more refinements.

In the United States, no one has dominated the field as much as Ron Arra, former professional baseball player and four-time winner of the national surf casting championship. Although his lifetime best cast in competition was 758.4 feet, no mean feat in itself, he once reached an astonishing 850 feet on the practice field, or almost three football fields laid end to end. Arra also became the first person to cast across the Cape Cod Canal (a famed striper hotspot). Flinging a weight those distances requires specialized gear. The tournament rod would not fish well, being far too stiff over most of its length. Conventional reels should have narrow spools, because less friction is generated as the line feeds through the first guide of the rod. Smooth monofilament line offers less resistance than braided line, the lighter the better, but to absorb the force of the cast without breaking, a heavier "shock" leader may be required.

But beyond appropriate gear is the essential need for power unleashed smoothly, with the correct technique. A number of long-distance casting styles have evolved, none as effective or as complicated as the pendulum cast. Invented by John Holden of the United Kingdom, the pendulum cast is not for the uncoordinated. Frank Daignault, in *Twenty Years on the Cape* (1989), writes of introducing Dave Docwra, the United Kingdom's distance-casting champion, in 1975 to American-style surf casting on Cape Cod. Docwra was from the East Anglian school of surf casters, an area where casting reached a high level of development in order to reach deep-sea fish from its gently sloping beaches. One British writer from elsewhere says, "The distances East Anglian anglers talk about when they are catching cod are like telephone numbers to us. I don't think I can see as far as some of those anglers cast."

One afternoon, Docwra put on an exhibition in front of dozens of surf casters, most of whom would be thrilled with a three-hundred-foot heave. His first throw—merely to wet the line—traveled 450 feet. He began his next cast forty-five feet from the water's edge, the purpose of which confused the gallery. Tossing the sinker away from the sea, he turned his body to follow the accelerating weight as he circled in a run, each leg braking his forward and turning motions as he traveled the distance to the sea. His fourteen-foot East Anglian rocket launcher, trailing thirteen feet of line, arced around his body; two fingers released the spool to travel at thirty-six thousand rpm; and the weight disappeared with a sound like a rifle shot, traveling about seven hundred feet. Needless to say, the locals were impressed.

LONGLINES AND LIGHT STICKS

One set would run from Washington, D.C., to Baltimore

Many cultures have used longlines—numerous hooks or gorges dangled from a main line. For the most part, these rigs extended for lengths of only feet or yards. But the scale of commercial longlining today is staggering. Some impressive statistics are reported in Linda Greenlaw's *The Hungry Ocean* (1999). Greenlaw captains the

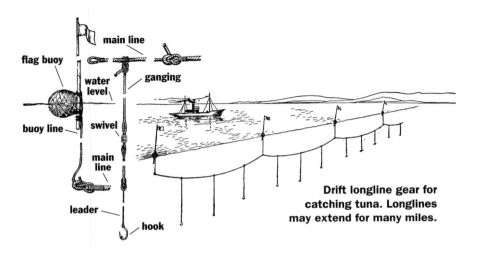

Drift longline gear for catching tuna. Longlines may extend for many miles.

Hannah Boden, a one-hundred-foot-long craft outfitted for one-month trips in search of swordfish, and a sister ship to the *Andrea Gail,* made famous as the ill-fated vessel lost in Sebastian Junger's *The Perfect Storm* (1997).

Before the *Hannah Boden* leaves the dock, twelve thousand pounds of squid are loaded on it as bait, as are miles of seven-hundred-pound-test main line, three thousand hooks, and eight thousand chemical light sticks in a variety of colors. Once far out at sea on the swordfish grounds, one set of a longline consists of 940-foot leaders and baited hooks snapped onto a remarkable forty miles of main line, with floats between every two leaders and an electronic beeper buoy (to provide the location) every fifty floats. Each of the leaders has a chemical light stick set six feet above the hook to attract baitfish and swordfish. A typical trip includes fifteen sets of this octopuslike gear and yields several hundred swordfish, dozens of bigeye tuna, and several mako sharks.

Another present-day oceanic longline fishery is found near Baffin Island for Greenland halibut. One difference is that it occurs under the ice. Inuit fishermen use a pulley to haul fish up from sixteen-hundred-foot depths. Their rigs involve a sliding rock weight, baited hooks, and a "kite" to catch the current to pull bottom line out.

A big problem with longlines around the world are that whales steal fish from them. In the Gulf of Alaska, sperm whales have learned to pluck sablefish off them "like grapes," according to one longliner, who says, "I don't know how they do it. . . . Sometimes you get the heads back, sometimes you just see lips, and sometimes they're just shredded."

Today fishermen who wish to light up their baits underwater have chemical sticks readily available. It was more difficult but nonetheless possible in 1590, when Leonard Mascall, in *A Book of Fishing with Hooke and Line, and All Other Instruments Thereunto Belonging,* prescribed a more primitive approach using glowworms, small worms that light up like fireflies along the banks of streams. He writes, "Ye shall distill in a lembeck of glasse, a quantitie of glowormes that shineth at night, with a soft fire, and out the distilled water into a thin vial of glasse, and thereunto put foure ounces of quicksilver." This was to be placed in a bow net and cast in the water, where the fish will "soone come unto the light, and covet to enter the net, and so ye shall take many."

LOOP-LINE FISHING

Lassoing fish in running water

Loop-lining is a major fishing method in Nepal that dates back about two centuries. It is distinguished from snaring done elsewhere in that it does not depend on the fisherman to visually place the loop around the fish.

The entire loop-lining kit includes a rod made of local reed, a rectangular piece of wood for a spool, wire rings to join the main nylon line to noose lines, and a sinker. The loops are made with a bamboo bar above them set to regulate the size of the opening. The loops traditionally were made from horsehair, but they were fragile and often failed to hold fish. In the early nineteenth century, thistle plant fibers were used, but today colored nylon thread is favored.

To fish a loop line, the rig is thrown into the water by swinging the rod in a gentle cast and letting the loops settle about three feet down in the water column. The single or multiple loops may be fished naked or adorned with colored material or bait as an attractant. Naked loops draw fish partly through their color and partly through the swimming action of the sinker and bamboo bar as they resist the current. Bait may consist of pounded wheat flour or chunks of yam, cucumber, gourd, or pumpkin. Midwater schooling fish investigate the rig, with one member eventually poking its snout and then its body through. Through these motions and the force of the fish's pectoral fins, the noose slides tighter, embracing the torso of the fish. As it struggles, its erect fins impede its escape. Sometimes the loop may instead wrap around the snout or one of the fins, nonetheless resulting in capture. Often a fish jumps to try to dislodge the loop while the fisherman pulls his catch toward the bank. Hefty fish may be taken this way, weighing as much as twenty pounds, with even larger ones usually breaking off.

Loop-line fishing is especially suited to fast-moving rivers, because fish of such ecosystems almost always are long-bodied, making snaring them far easier than if they were round in profile. But not all species respond similarly. Bottom feeders do not enter the gear, nor do fish that have barbels, such as catfish. But many fish do, including the revered game fish mahseer.

M

MAMMALS AS FISH BAITS

Sometimes the tables turn

Although it happens far more frequently the other way around, some fish are large enough to consume mammals. Big old brown trout in rivers may begin to disdain insects in favor of meals that come in larger packages, including other trout, as well as mice and shrews that attempt to swim over their lairs. Anglers who stay on streams after dark to pursue these outsize browns clip off their size 16 and 18 dry flies, replacing them with bushy offerings that resemble small rodents and have more affinity with the husky hair flies often used for largemouth bass.

In Mongolia, large rivers are lorded over by the largest member of the salmon family, the taimen, a piscine submarine that can reach two hundred pounds and will rise and smash small mammals crossing above their lies. In what may be the ultimate perversion of dry-fly fishing, anglers tie a hook to a live squirrel and drag the squirming, floating rodent across the top of a pool where a taimen has been observed. Actual fly fishermen cast a monstrous bundle of feathers known as a Mongolian Swimming Mouse. Indians in western Canada used a downsized version of the live-mammal technique with real mice for outsize rainbow trout.

Pike rule the warm-water ponds and lakes of northern Europe, eating anything smaller than they are. In the sixteenth century, John

Taverner wrote that a pike "will hardly feed on anything except it stirre and be alive," which doesn't rule out much. An 1853 *Fraser's Magazine* article reports, "Amongst a great variety of *objets de consommation* the following have been ascertained to be most to their taste—a swan's head and shoulders, a mule's lip, a Polish damsel's foot, a gentleman's hand (probably, however, no objection would be made to a lady's); plump puppies just opening their eyes, and tender kittens paying the penalty of a mother's indiscretion; together with every kind of fish that comes to the maw, with the few exceptions just noticed." One British writer found a rat inside a pike he caught, and it is worth noting that the record pike in Ireland—a full-bellied fifty-three-pounder—contained a ten-pound salmon.

Other fish besides salmonids and pike may eat warm-blooded animals. Someone told a friend of mine about fishing under the George Washington Bridge over the Hudson River when he was young. At least twice, rats that were living among the rocks got swept into the river. Their struggles caught the attention of large striped bass, which finished them off.

MECHANICAL DEVICES

Patent Office rejects?

Besides large mechanical devices to catch fish, such as fish wheels, there are numerous smaller forms of inventive hardware, only a few of which are taken seriously. Drum gravity traps are used in Guiana and Niger. This is a variant of the old American schoolboy trick for trapping squirrels. In the African version, a weighted bamboo reed cylinder is suspended so that as soon as a fish pulls at the bait, the cylinder falls and traps the fish.

Swedes use a spring shutter trap for pike fishing. A small fish is fitted as bait to a horizontal hook. As soon as a pike strikes, the spring releases and a sharp spike impales this fish's head, either gripping or killing it.

Europeans have used traps that operate like bear traps, springing shut when tripped. But instead of paired iron jaws, these traps have net bags so as not to harm the fish. They were used on the

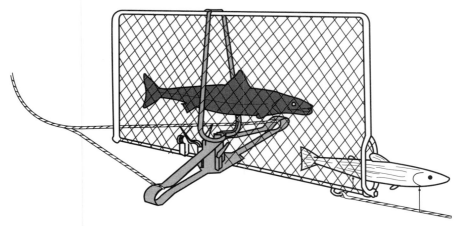

Salmon trap from the upper Rhine with a wooden fish serving as an attractant.

upper Rhine with either live salmon or wooden dummies to draw victims. Across the Atlantic, bear traps actually have been used to catch fish. A Nova Scotia poacher told a friend of mine that he used Conibear traps on poles and bumped them on the noses of Atlantic salmon to spring them. The trap snaps over the fish's head, killing it.

The concept of the automatic hooksetter has fired the imagination of many a U.S. patent dreamer, but these always seem to end up as interesting gimmicks that no one actually uses. One is meant for bank fishing and is built around a spring-loaded rod holder that trips when it senses a strike. Hooksetters have even been incorporated into floating bobbers, one model being advertised as "the bobber with a brain." Its inventor may have been thinking just a bit too hard.

MIDGES AND MICROFLIES

Squinting helps

Midges are absurdly small, mosquitolike aquatic insects that are just large enough to attract and, because they often occur in huge numbers, dominate a trout's attention. Colloquial names may include punkies, gnats, no-see-ums, and smuts, but true midges are not biting bugs and only annoy people in other ways: by swarming around their faces and by making trout nearly impossible to catch.

Trout eat midges at three of their life stages: as pupae, larvae, and flying adults. Although pupae may be green, black, brown, or red, and the other two stages also vary in color by species, finding the right fly color is not important, but matching its size is critical. When you are using a regular fly and not catching rising trout, but some are striking the knots in your leaders, consider it time to try midging.

Midge fishing can be the ultimate fly-fishing frustration: biblical numbers of insects being preyed upon by eager trout, yet nary a take. A. J. McClane, in his classic *Standard Fishing Encyclopedia* (1965), typically understates this when he writes, "Periodically, salmonids consume vast quantities of midges, and the fly-fisher must be prepared to cope with the situation, as trout often show great selectivity at these times." It's estimated that on average, a trout needs to eat about 3 percent of its weight in food each day to survive. If so, then it may take five hundred midges to satisfy a two-pound trout.

One fly fisher on New Mexico's San Juan River encountered hundreds of big trout sipping from millions of midges on the river surface, but he described it not as paradise, but as hell. So dense were the tiny bugs that he likened the water as having grown a five o'clock shadow. (Others have called it "black velvet.") Try as he might after a cast, he could not distinguish his own fly from the multitudes of real ones surrounding it, at times striking at fish that had taken the real thing eighteen inches from his own offering. After a full day of not drawing a take in the midst of nonstop rises, the angler knelt and, on a low angle with a short cast, saw that even with an ultrafine leader, the minuscule fly could not float as "free as the truths that slid along the current beside it."

To imitate these microbugs, anglers tie flies on hooks as small as the infinitesimal size 32, for which a magnifying glass is needed while working. Because midge densities can be so high, they often interlock legs and other body parts, forming "midge clusters." In order to be able to present a larger, meatier offering, some anglers fish cluster fly patterns that resemble little heaps of midges.

There also is one last challenge with midging. Because the leaders used are so fine—about the diameter of a hair—a problem is learning not to break the trout off at the strike when you are fortunate to receive one.

N

NIGHT KNIFE-FISHING

A strangely alluring sport

The seemingly crude technique of whacking fish with a knife as they swim is actually regarded as high sport in Nepal, where it is seen as a measure of one's wit and skill in manipulating a blade. "No sport is more alluring than this," writes one Nepalese practitioner.

The *khukari*, or Nepal knife, is a curved, almost swordlike weapon. Originally *khukari* fishing in the dark of night was aided by burning chips of wood bathed in tree gum, under the belief that this light source also had an odor that attracted fish. But more recently, lanterns and torches have been used to attract and bewilder potential targets. This fishing is carried out during the dry season, when stream waters are low and clear,

The crude but culturally important Nepalese method of hunting fish with knives at night aided by torchlight.

and in the darkness of the week before or after the new moon to maximize the shocking effect on the fish of a burst of light. The knife wielder works with a team: two fish collectors and one or two light holders. When a fish is seen, he aims for its head. And when a concentration of fish is found, he slices the sharp knife quickly back and forth to maximize strikes.

NIGHT LIGHTS

Bright ideas

One way that marine researchers catch deep-sea organisms that would be difficult to capture by any other means is by lighting the surface of the sea and waiting to see what emerges from the darkness below. Indeed, this can be the most exciting part of a research cruise. Squid and various small baitfish usually show. But by using dip nets in the illuminated area, scientifically important juvenile specimens of many large fish, such as marlins and lancetfish, have been taken.

Night lights are routinely used on angling headboats that fish overnight at sea. When done correctly, the illuminated area around the vessel may have a mix of baitfish and squid that draws tuna and dolphinfish. Lights may also be used creatively for survival or augmentation fishing. Off Mombasa, the crew of a destroyer on a thirty-day cruise and tired of navy grub simply hung a lamp off a gun turret, resulting in flying fish all over the deck.

Night-light fishing is not without its hazards, though. The needlefish and houndfish that are gathered purposely in places by torchlight may leap and wound the vessel's crew. And once while dip-netting from the dive platform of a research vessel at a night-light station, a scientist moved with uncommon speed when a large sea snake slithered up to his feet.

NOODLING FOR CATFISH

It takes getting a feel for

Noodling is a remarkably direct approach practiced in the South and Midwest, where fishermen feel for large catfish in holes in lakes and creeks, with the fish latching on to the noodler's hand—or vice versa. As with many arcane practices in the United States, the terminology is regionalized: In Mississippi, Alabama, and North Carolina, it's called grabbling; in Arkansas and Missouri, hogging; in Nebraska, stumping; in Georgia, cooning; and in Kentucky, dogging. The origin of its Texas and Oklahoma name, noodling, is unknown, but one theory is that it derives from the slippery nature of catfish, which feel like a wet noodle. Its official name, according to many state wildlife regulations booklets, is hand fishing. Native Hawaiians also noodled, pulling fish out of holes in coral reefs with their fingers, but it's highly unlikely they called it that.

Noodling in North America apparently began with its natives, but as one writer notes, unlike with fishhooks or nets, noodling leaves no archaeological traces. But there is the written record. In *History of the American Indians* (1775), James Adair described a similar technique to noodling, in which the men wrapped their breeches or other fabric around one arm down to the hand, and then dived under rock ledges to present the cloth bait to large catfish. When the fish seized the bait, the diver opened his hand and grabbed the fish, and then wrestled it to shore.

The rules for noodling are simple: Never noodle alone, because you could be kept underwater by a strong catfish or a snag. Know how to swim. And wear as little clothing as possible, to minimize the chances of its getting caught on submerged branches. Some noodlers probe holes first with a stick. They know that if the occupant feels rough, it's a snake; if it feels like a rock, it's a turtle; and if it feels smooth, it's probably a catfish. Bad luck if it's an alligator snapping turtle—they've been known to trim a noodler's fingers.

Huge catfish are landed this way. A book by Burkhard Bilger titled *Noodling for Flatheads* (2000) contains a chapter on it, which prompted a highly entertaining documentary film called *Okie Noodling*. Bilger became aware of noodling when he noticed that one of his Oklahoma high school classmates bore faint scars along his forearm, which Bilger learned were from the teeth of flathead catfish. Flatheads and blue catfish are true midwestern sea monsters; Bilger says that "according to one old story, when pioneer mothers did their wash by a stream, they sometimes heard a splash and a muffled yelp: where a little boy had been playing, only a few bubbles were left." The Oklahoma state record flathead weighed 73 pounds; the record blue, 111 pounds.

Fortunately for noodlers, catfish lack true fangs, but they do have coarse teeth designed to keep food moving in, not out. They also have a tendency to spin when clamped on an arm, causing one noodler to describe the feeling like a pencil sharpener. "Once that thing gets to flouncin', and that sandpaper gets to rubbin', it can peel your hide plumb off," he says.

Part of the allure of noodling is that it's a damned hard challenge. Beyond the physical requirements of diving and groping in muddy water, "hookups" don't always result in catches—the catfish often wins. For his master's thesis at Mississippi State University, one aspiring fisheries biologist spent three years noodling on two rivers. The statistics were not flattering; he landed thirty-five catfish in 1,362 tries, or one fish for every 39 noodles. "I can't tell you how tough it was," he later said to Bilger. "Some of those fish were incredibly, incredibly vicious."

Finding the fish, if not actually landing them, can be made easier by seeding the bottom with attractive homes. Some noodlers place sawed-off oil barrels or other structures on the catfish grounds. One Arkansas pond has such well-made catfish dens that it's called the "hole-tel." But purists still prefer to grope under natural rock caves and sunken detritus.

The film *Okie Noodling* featured some earthy noodlers who made up with gumption what they lacked in teeth. It's been said that "the perfect noodler has arms six feet long, a lot of grit, no brains, and hails from Oklahoma, Texas, or Iowa." But noodling has some fair-haired aficionados, such as Kristi Addis, Miss Teen USA 1987, who told the judges at the pageant, in what surely was a first for the event, that one of her favorite pastimes is grabbling for flatheads on the Yalobusha.

A more recent film, *Mississippi Handgrabbing*, also popularizes the glories of hand fishing for catfish, with the catchy come-on that "these guys bring a whole new meaning to the words 'I've got a bite! They literally mean—I've got a bite.'"

NOOSING SHARKS

Not for cowards

Only the most accomplished Melanesian fishermen practiced *oungeuaol*, the capture of sharks in open ocean waters. At the request of their chiefs, these men would sail offshore looking for floating driftwood, around which they knew several species of sharks often congregated. Vibrations from coconut shells shaken underwater also were a powerful draw for sharks. When a shark approached, it was pulled nearer using a white stone attached to a line as a kind of artificial lure. When the shark was very close, flying fish were used as a hand-held attractant. But because lines made from plant fibers could not long resist a shark's teeth, islanders instead learned to noose the fish. Placement around the gills was best, because they offered a good holdfast and because it slowed the fish's respiration. Speedier tuna could also be caught by tossing chum around the boat to attract them, and then noosing them in front of their stiff tails.

A more distant but equally skillful application was to noose sharks at depths of as much as sixty to eighty fathoms, obviously a tactile rather than visual operation. To do this, a bait was suspended by fine lines to a heavy, stiff noose. Based on feel, the fisherman reared back on the line, hoping to loop the shark between its pectoral and dorsal fins.

Oungeuaol fishing was considered prestigious, not because sharks were so esteemed as food, but because of the danger involved. Many sharks were six to eight feet in length. One practitioner had a special tattoo on his wrist. When holding out the flying fish to draw a shark, he was not supposed to drop the bait until the tip of the shark's snout reached the tattoo.

Much ritual was attached to this prestigious form of fishing. Months of labor were invested in preparation for a special celebration upon completion of the trip. Tropical almonds were mixed with coconut syrup and starch to be made into edible shark sculptures as long as eight feet. And sexual intercourse was forbidden prior to the expedition. Because of that taboo, fisherman today are said to be glad that *oungeuaol* fishing died out about a century ago.

OLD WORLD STURGEON SNAGGING

Latching on to giants

The world's sturgeons are predictable fish in that when they are not at sea, they usually are found on the channel bottoms of large rivers. But despite this knowledge, it is not easy to net them in these places because of their strong currents and considerable depths. In Europe and Asia, hook-and-line fisheries developed for sturgeon—but not of the usual kind. No bait is used. Instead, arrays of special hooks called *samolovs* are soaked to snag the ancient behemoths; *samolov* means "automatic catcher."

Not only do the hooks remain unbaited, but they are fished upside down, with the line attached to the inner bend and tied to a surface float to keep the position reversed. Material for floats has included willow, pine, and lombardy bark and cork, with the float also serving as something of an attractant. To make them even more enticing, some were fitted with feathers. The effectiveness of the approach is not in doubt; less certain is the reason why it works. One theory is that sturgeon feed by lashing food toward their mouths with their tails, in the process impaling themselves. Another is that sturgeon are frolicsome creatures that like to play with objects they encounter. Regardless, most are caught with *samolovs* either near the fish's tail or under its pelvic fins, although for some reason the small sterlet species often is hooked in its anus.

121

The approach extends way back in history, with one form of snagging hook made of bone known from the Mesolithic age, roughly ten thousand years ago. Indeed, some believe that the Neolithic colonization of European river valleys was greatly aided by seasonal sturgeon fisheries of this kind. Sturgeon have been revered across their range, especially the largest species. The giant beluga, known to reach four and a half tons, was protected under special royal grants in Russia and Hungary. In China, only the emperor had the right to consume the Chinese sturgeon, whose Chinese name means "imperial fish." In the United Kingdom, according to Charles Dickens in *A Dictionary of the Thames* (1883), any sturgeon caught "was not to be secreted," and all royal fish taken within the jurisdiction of the lord mayor of London, which included whales, porpoises, sturgeon, and "such like," were to be sent directly to grace the table of majesty.

Sturgeon snagging hooks actually are quite small in relation to the sometimes impressive size of the fish. But diminutive

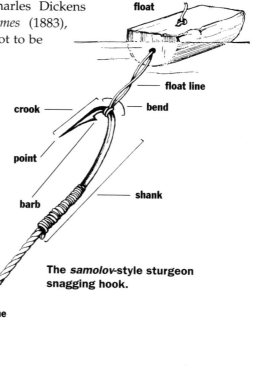

The *samolov*-style sturgeon snagging hook.

hooks suffice because, even though they may not bury deep into the fish's tough hide, most sturgeon are remarkably passive when snagged or restrained by any other means, such as nets. One writer described their resistance as "less than that of algae."

These hooks are fished in various ways. Aelianus, a writer of the second and third centuries, provides a detailed description of a beluga sturgeon fishing episode in the Balkans. In his account, a fisherman drives a pair of oxen to the bank of the Ister. He then fastens a strong rope to the middle of the yoke and amply feeds the oxen. To the other end of the rope, he attaches a strong and sharp hook, which he spikes through the lung of a bull, after fastening a piece of lead to the rope to keep it from being carried away from the bottom. As soon as the fish becomes aware of the bull's meat, it darts to seize it. As it takes it and splashes happily about, it impales itself on the *samolov*. Apparently not quiescent after being hooked, the sturgeon "agitates thirstily and shakes the rope with great force," at which time the fisherman jumps up and drives his oxen, eventually dragging the fish ashore. This passage has been translated such that the fish is the giant European catfish, and not the sturgeon. But one scholar's thorough analysis makes a strong case for its being a sturgeon and says that one of the purposes of the bull lung was to serve as a float to keep the snagging hook in the correct upside-down position.

Sturgeon snagging evolved over time into a variety of manifestations, many of which included numerous hooks set in a row. One approach in the Danube

Fishing for giant sturgeon on the Danube with the aid of animals (reconstructed after the description of Aelianus).

for beluga was a series of tridentate hooks fished upright and dangled off a rope that wound its way across bundles of branches used as floats in the current. Tridentate hooks also were fished upside down, using a cork at their base to float them off a sunken line below. Yet another variation was to hang *samolov* hooks off poles placed in the bottom in an alternating fashion as a gauntlet for passing beluga. A sturgeon needed to be careful where it swam in the Danube.

OTTER FISHING

Amiable and well-trained assistants

River otters are among the most playful, agile, and intelligent mammals in existence. They can remain submerged for two minutes and are so comfortable underwater that Izaak Walton thought them a species of fish. Resembling large weasels, wild otters also are consummate fish catchers. When trained, they can catch fish at rapid rates.

Like cormorant fishing, otter fishing was developed long ago in China. In fact, one Chinese observer wrote that a fisherman would no more be without an otter than a hunter without a dog. More than six hundred years ago, Marco Polo observed Chinese fishing with otters in the Yangtze River. Friar Odoric reported on this practice in 1513: "They fish by means of another fish called a diver. They keep it by a cord attached to a fine collar. It has a muzzle and neck like a fox, forepaws like a dog, hind feet like a duck and the body of a fish. It dives into the water and I swear in less than two hours it had filled two big baskets, always depositing the fish in the baskets." Otters also were used in India, in the Rivers Indus, Ganges, and elsewhere in Bengal, and also in bays along the Cochin Coast.

Otter training was introduced into Europe in the sixteenth century. Isaak Walton mentions it in his *Compleat Angler,* written in 1653. If pups were caught and trained at an age of three or four months, he says, they became very tame and trusting and might provide fifteen or more years of active fishing. In Sweden, whole families were supported by a trained otter, with some fishermen selling their more traditional gear as unnecessary. One observer said he saw an otter so perfectly trained that it would corner a school of fish in a pool, and then pick out any one that his master indicated. King James I kept domesticated otters at Westminster for his amusement. Otters were used in Europe as late as the 1880s, but because they were so often used by poachers to catch salmon, it became illegal to tame them, and the practice of otter fishing perished in the Western world.

P

PILCHARD RINGS

Fish see red and charge

No one is sure why this Florida specialty works, but pilchard rings do catch pilchards, small herrings or sardines popular as baitfish. A pilchard ring is kind of like a mini gill net fished on a rod and reel or off a hand-held rope, except that the gill net is actually a single strand of wire loops with a weight attached to the lowest ring. The key to the ensemble is that a red wool thread must be wound through the rings.

Pilchard rings are most effectively fished off piers. If the fisherman sees a concentration of pilchards, he drops the rig among them; otherwise, it may be fished blind. For some reason, the pilchards are attracted to the wool thread, and many of these fish pass their heads through the rings, becoming unable to back out and hence are gilled in the process.

Pilchard rings may become loaded with pilchards—a chain gang of sorts—attracting cormorants in the process. Cormorants are such fish lovers that they may hang on to the pilchard rig as it's being retrieved. One angler lifted a bird four feet out of the water before it let go.

Because this is a visually based fish-catching approach, pilchard ring fishing is purely a daytime affair. The size of the rings is crucial. They must match the size of the available pilchards, so some anglers hedge their bets by joining a series of rings of different sizes.

PIT TRAPS

A falling tide lowers all fish

Tide waits for neither man nor fish. But man has learned to use tide to his advantage in catching fish. Beyond anglers learning which tides produce the best harvests, tides can be used to leave fish high and dry.

In Indochina, fishermen use bag nets, made from mesh stretched loosely among four stationary poles, to take advantage of changes in water height. Fish enter at high tide but are left suspended—and bewildered—as the water drops. American researchers of fish in wetlands use a similar strategy. For example, the ecological value of the common reed phragmites has been debated where it occurs along the East Coast. To help resolve this question, scientists have examined fish utilization of these areas. But because phragmites stands flood only at the highest stages of the tide, and then only minimally, and because of their dense growth, traditional seining techniques can't be used. The answer is pit traps—shallow pockets are dug, with plastic cups fitted at their lowest points. These areas concentrate killifish and other small fish at high water, and then leave them impounded during the ebb, allowing them to be counted and measured.

POISONING

A chemical death

Carl Safina writes in a *Song for the Blue Ocean* (1997) about how commercial poisoning in tropical waters is decimating fish stocks and killing off coral reefs in the process. Poisoning in and of itself is not always destructive; it's a matter of the details of application and of scale. In parts of the Pacific, there is a long history of using natural poisons, such as those found in sea cucumbers, to kill fish, but this was done by local artisanal fisheries that caused little environmental harm.

Today sodium cyanide, the same compound used to execute prisoners, is widely used by divers to capture exotic tropical marine fish for the aquarium trade. Holding squirt bottles containing a cyanide solution, they release the chemical into caves and holes in coral reefs to stun their quarry. Cyanide cripples enzyme systems involved in respiration, and exposure to it damages the liver, stomach, intestines, and reproductive organs; indeed, it is so deadly that divers who swam through clouds of their own poison have been killed. Some fish die immediately, but those living specimens selected are brought to holding areas to recuperate. Many of these appear to have recovered, but then succumb to long-term effects weeks later, back in aquariums.

The environmental effects of this illegal and immoral fishery are enormous. Not only are fish killed, but great expanses of coral are too. Large coral heads may be hundreds of years old. Unfortunately, coral is extremely sensitive to cyanide, with laboratory tests showing fatality at concentrations two hundred thousand times lower than those in fishermen's squirt bottles. An active cyanide user doses about fifty coral heads per day, perhaps 225 days a year. It's estimated that in the Philippines alone, three thousand cyanide users squirt tens of millions of coral heads each year. And this environmentally devastating fishing technique has spread throughout much of the tropical Indo-Pacific.

Fresh waters are not immune from the poison scourge. Today in Russia, poachers pour pounds of chloride of lime (bleaching powder) into streams. The "fishermen" collect stricken fish with dip nets as they move downstream with the polluted water. Typical catches in swift Russian streams and brooks include grayling, trout, and chub. Some Russian poachers also add chlorine at strategic locations upstream to drive grayling and taimen into nets.

Before the rampant misuse of intensely poisonous chemicals, aborigines all over the world used milder poisons in sustainable fashion; some still do. Native Americans such as the Catawba, Cherokee, and Delaware mashed black walnuts with quartzite hammerstones, and then tossed the mush upstream in flowing water. This compound acted as a neurotoxin, temporarily paralyzing the fish, and it was effective in shallow northeastern streams and creeks in gathering suckers, chub, and brook trout. The Creek tribe used horse chestnuts similarly. In Guyana, the Carib Indians made balls of bait from cassava mixed with the toxin-laced leaves of *Clibadium*. They tossed the small balls into the river, where the fish swallowed the balls whole. The stupefied fish floated to the surface for easy capture.

The Jivaros in South America used barbasco, a jungle vine, for their poison. A great pile of the plant was mashed to pulp on the rocks. After fishermen stationed themselves downstream, about two to three hundred pounds of the mash were thrown into the river. The fish die and float belly up. So potent was this poison that fish may have been stricken as far as three miles downstream. Likewise, Australian aborigines released the sap of the milky mangrove to poison river fish.

Palauans poisoned fish in shallow tidepools using a red liquid obtained by rubbing the skin of the sea cucumber. This compound also encouraged octopuses to leave their lairs for open waters, where they could be speared. The Palauans also used derris root and other poisonous plants to kill reef fish, but wisely, they were taught to avoid placing it near living coral, which could succumb, as well.

Poisons have been used for some highly specialized applications. A blind species of molly has evolved in the underwater cave of a river in Tapijulapa, Mexico. Although mollies are most often associated with tropical freshwater fish hobbyists, this particular molly holds religious significance for local Indians. To capture the mollies, they drop a poisonous plant into the waters just inside the cave. This kills some of the fish, which are then carried out of the cave and subsequently used in a fertility-related rite. When fishing pools disappeared after water was diverted, Nepalese fishermen used ichthyotoxic juices of about half a dozen native plants, which caused the impounded fish to become somewhat blinded and restless and to jump often.

The poisoning of fish also figures in classical and early western literature. Aristotle writes of poisoning tuna by lowering cakes made of cyclamen and clay. The Greek Oppian provides a colorful description of the piscine workings of cyclamen:

> Soon as the deadly Cyclamen invades
> The ill-starred fishes in their deep-sunk glades,
> . . . the slowly working bane
> Creeps o'er each sense and poisons every vein,
> Then pours concentrated mischief on the brain,
> Some drugged, like men o'ercome with recent wine,
> Reel to and fro, and stagger thro' the brine;
> Some in quick circlets whirl: some 'gainst the rocks
> Dash, and are stunned by repercussive shocks;
> Some with quenched orbs, or filmy eyeballs thick,
> Rush on the nets and in the meshes stick,
> In coma steeped their fins more feebly ply,
> Some in titanic spasms gasp and die.
> Soon as the splashings cease and stillness reigns,
> The jocund crew collect, and count their gains.

In *The Art of Angling* (1774), Charles Bowlker discusses many combinations of plants and compounds that poison fish. He says the best method is to gather *Baccae piscatoriae*, also called "fisher's berries," and pound them into a mortar; make them into balls of paste about the size of a pea; and then throw them into standing water. According to Bowlker, the fish that taste it will become intoxicated and will rise and lie on the surface of the water. But Bowlker does not suggest that these methods actually be used; he presents them in order to help detect poachers, concluding after providing a recipe that includes goat's blood and lungs that "this, however, as well as other unfair practices, is seldom resorted to by a generous Angler."

POLING FOR MULLET

Thinning the ranks on the sly

Poling is an old British mullet-fishing technique that continued on a commercial scale into the mid-twentieth century. To get the notoriously shy mullet to bite, an area was chummed for days or weeks with mashed fish, oil, and blood. The fisherman then used a twelve-foot-long bamboo pole with a short line tied to it. Because mullet are so shy, the skilled poler needed to hook and swing them out of the water in one motion, even though they could run as large as nine pounds, so that the rest of the school remained unaware that their numbers were dwindling. If poling is practiced today, it's purely for nostalgia's sake.

PUDDLING

Bubbles kill

Puddling is an aboriginal technique used in swampy waters. These highly organic habitats usually have sediments in which noxious gases are held; worldwide, these gases often escape and can be seen bubbling to the surface. Tribal people in locations as distant as Guyana and Nepal stomp through the shallows to stir up mud and release poisonous gases such as methane, hydrogen sulfide, and ammonia. They also may drag a heavy stone or log through the mud to assist the process. These compounds narcotize the fish, which then can be easily scooped up.

PUTCHER RANKS

Fish cornucopias

Atlantic salmon excite anglers as they flash in the depths of often gin-clear rivers. I've watched spawners hold in the pellucid currents of Nova Scotia's Margaree River, where the highly visible but reticent fish drove anglers mad. To get to these transparent reaches, salmon must swim through typically murky estuaries—places where fresh water blends with seawater—at the river mouths. The Severn River estuary in Wales, with its forty-eight-foot tides generating strong currents, is especially silty. There, long ago, commercial fishermen devised ingenious basket weirs known as putcher ranks to make use of the poor visibility to fool the salmon.

A putcher is a five- to fourteen-foot-long conical basket similar in appearance to an ice cream cone. Putchers are placed in stands and stacked four high in a rank. They were long constructed from highly flexible willow and hazel, but by the mid-1990s, most were made of aluminum. In their heyday, eleven thousand individual putchers were licensed on the Severn, with between fifty and twenty-four hundred baskets at any one location. Most were fished facing upstream to catch salmon and other species dropping downriver on the ebbing tide. Fish entering the funnel would reach the tapered end and be unable to turn around and exit. Fishermen harvest their catches as the tide recedes, leaving the baskets empty to fish again on the next ebb tide.

The earliest records of putcher ranks date to 1113, in association with the founding of a Benedictine monastery, but this form of fishing stretches back at least three millennia. This fact is known because in 1990, a local archaeologist stumbled across ancient remains of similar fish traps on the Severn shores; carbon dating showed them to be three thousand years old. The last remaining putcher ranks on the Severn are of the Goldcliff Fisheries. How much longer the Severn salmon fishery will last is unclear. Most Atlantic salmon stocks, including those of the Severn, are severely depleted, and one of the most powerful tools of restoration has been the buying out of local and high-seas fisheries. The Severn's putcher ranks, after at least three thousand years of continuous operation, have been bought out for five years. Another three millennia into the future of salmon fishing with putcher ranks appears rather unlikely.

R

RAKING HERRING AND SETTING FOR HERRING ROE

More fun than raking leaves

Pacific herring once ran inshore in unfathomable numbers to spawn in coves along the Alaskan and British Columbian coasts of North America. So dense were these spawning aggregations that Indians in canoes could simply swish a rake through the water to harvest them. But some rakes worked better than others. Different tribes had their own variations, but the basic herring rake consisted of a long, rounded wooden pole fitted with a row of many perpendicular or backswept teeth on its working end. Regardless of style, it was no small task to construct these rakes. The teeth usually were barbs made of sharpened splinters of deer bone. Waterproofing of the apparatus involved smoking it over a fire for four days and rubbing in tallow each morning to make the soot adhere as a sealant.

The herring run lasted only about twenty days, but what food was landed! The rake was drawn through the water with a paddle-like motion, up and under the fish. One observer writes, "It is astonishing to see how many are caught by those dextrous at this kind of fishing, as they seldom fail, when shoals are numerous, of taking as many as ten or twelve at a stroke, and in a very short time will fill a canoe with them." And it wasn't difficult to pull them off the tines—a rap of the rake on the gunwale, and the hold would fill.

Such vast numbers of herring spawning in tight quarters produced voluminous quantities of eggs. Today these same herring are eagerly sought by large commercial netting operations for their roe, which is cut out of the fish's bodies. But Northwest Coast Indians let the herring do the work, setting roe catchers in the form of spruce or fir boughs weighted with stones to hang vertically. After several days, they retrieved the branches, now laden with a thick coating of eggs, to be air dried and eaten for the remainder of the year.

READING THE BIRDS

Their bills point toward the fish

In New England and along the mid-Atlantic coast, anglers know that dense flocks of terns, gulls, or gannets usually signal striped bass or bluefish ravaging a baitfish school below. The seabirds capitalize on the carnage, picking off distracted or wounded prey. On the fall run of game fish down the Atlantic coast, some surf casters do nothing but look for "birds working," with the knowledge that finding them almost guarantees great fishing. In these places, such scenes are known as blitzes, short for the German *blitzkrieg,* or lightning strike; elsewhere around the world, they may be called feeding frenzies or munch ups.

But nowhere has watching the birds reached a greater degree of refinement than in Palau, where for centuries, fishermen have searched for these aerial indicators. Because of their keen eyesight and their perspective from on high, seabirds can see and track fish schools that are deep below the surface (the deeper the fish dive, the higher up the birds fly above them to gain better views). Predatory fish species differ in the speed and pattern of their search for food, and these differences are mirrored in the movements of the birds tracking them. Different species of fish also focus on different size ranges of prey, as do different bird species. By watching the birds, an experienced fisherman can not only tell where the fish are, but also can gain some sense of their identity, whether they are actively feeding, and sometimes even what they are feeding on.

If flocks of black noddy tern are seen quartering a few feet above the surface, then feeding briefly before flying off hundreds of yards to feed again, it indicates that they are following skipjack tuna. If these same birds are flying over feeding yellowfin tuna, their movements are slower, with fewer changes in direction. Schools of yellowfin and the flocks that hover over them also are more likely to break into adjacent subgroups. But if these birds move even more slowly, over water more heavily churned, it suggests the presence of kawa kawa *(Euthynnus affinis)*. Birds flying high and slowly without diving may be following a school of tuna in deep water, waiting for it to surface and feed.

If a few birds are diving sporadically, this indicates species that don't form large schools, such as wahoo, barracuda, or Spanish mackerel. But if these birds are feeding a mile or more off the reef, these three inshore fish species probably can be ruled out.

When a flock of feeding noddies breaks up, it means that the fish have dived. The fisherman may then look high for white terns, which fly higher than noddies or shearwaters and, with their superior vantage point, often are the first to reach newly surfacing fish.

In New England waters, diving gulls always signify feeding game fish, whereas diving terns may fool anglers, because these birds are nimble enough to catch baitfish on their own with nary a striper or bluefish present. In Lapland, small marine birds known as sea swallows were of great assistance during salmon season and were called the "luck bringers." For some reason, they follow the inward and outward course of the fish, serving as infallible guides to the fishermen.

REEF-NETTING SALMON

Fake underwater jungles beguile

Reef netting is an old means of netting salmon by Northwest Coast Indians. A somewhat rectangular net with a rise at its far end was set on the bottom over a kelp-covered reef. This net, which was

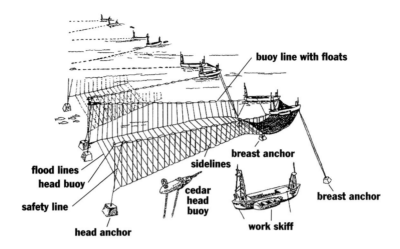

considered female in the Indian culture, had a hole in its middle which to them represented a vulva. Salmon moved toward the net via a pathway cut through the kelp bed, while rows of fishermen in two parallel canoes watched through the clear water. When enough salmon were above the net, they lifted it quickly in unison, bagging the fish and then retrieving them through the hole. In deeper water without kelp, side and bottom lines, sometimes with vegetation tied in, were used to steer salmon toward the net.

Today's reef netting modernizes an old Native American concept for catching salmon. This "community" approach is practiced only around the straits and bays of the Lummi and San Juan Islands of the Pacific Northwest. Fishermen build artificial reefs at adjacent sites with ropes festooned with weeds or "sea camouflage" to form an area of attractive fish habitat similar to a large kelp bed. Each imitation reef leads directly into a net held between two fishing boats, each equipped with observation towers. Observers watch in the clear water for salmon schools attracted to the reef to cross the outer edge of the net. Once the fish are spotted, the fishermen haul in their surprised catches.

REMORAS: LIVING FISHHOOKS

Piscine suction cups

Remoras are sleek, striped fish that have what looks like an oval of comblike rows on top of the head. This strange adaptation is really a sucker disk that allows the remora to clamp on to large sea creatures to hitch rides. When the shark, billfish, ray, or sea turtle it is riding on kills a meal, the remora detaches to pick up scraps.

The potential to enlist remoras as fish catchers did not escape the Arawak Indians of southern Cuba, as first reported in 1504 by Peter Martyr, who learned of it directly from Columbus. According to Martyr, the Arawaks kept a supply of live remoras, which they called *guaicanum*, in shallow-water pens. When the fishermen spotted sea turtles near shore, they released a suckerfish with a line tied around its tail. The remora would clamp on to the turtle so tightly that the fishermen could pull both fish and reptile back to the boat or shore.

Unfortunately for Martyr, he was strongly ridiculed in Rome for insisting that the story was true. But suckerfish had long held a place in mythology. Among these stories was their role in the death of Emperor Caligula, in which they were said to have fastened to his vessel and held it back, allowing enemy ships to overtake it. Mark Antony's defeat at Actium also was reportedly caused by remoras holding back his galley.

Martyr was vindicated posthumously when reputable eighteenth- and nineteenth-century explorers returned home with stories of natives using remoras as fishing tools in remote areas such as Zanzibar, India, Malaysia, Japan, the South Pacific, and South America. Modifications to the approach reported by Martyr were found. Australian aborigines ran a cord through a hole pierced through the stem of the remora's tail. In other areas, the line was fastened to a ring placed around the base of the tail. Some fishermen ran a second line through the remora's mouth and gills, then slung the fish over the side of the boat. The forward line kept the fish's head facing the current so that it could respire, and it also kept the remora from fastening to the bottom of the boat. In still other areas, the fishermen let the captive remora ride on the hull, but kept a bamboo pole ready to dislodge the fish when it was needed.

The remora's most remarkable feature, its suction disk, is derived from its dorsal fin. As the fish evolved, the spines of the fin divided and flattened out, becoming a plate with movable parts that operate like slats of a Venetian blind. Over time, this modification moved forward on the body until it reached the top surface of the head. But this did not occur recently; a fossil suckerfish from sixty million years ago had a suction disk like those found today. The holding power of these disks are incredible. In a test at the New York Aquarium, a bucket of water weighing twenty-four and a half pounds was lifted into the air by a line attached to a remora. A forty-pound sailfish was almost lifted from the deck of a boat using a four-inch specimen, and it might have been raised completely if the remora's disk hadn't torn off.

Although many native fishermen used remoras to fish with, not all of them treated their living fishhooks with the same regard. Although West Indian practitioners sang songs of praise to their hunting fish, Australian aborigines simply ate them afterward.

ROTENONE AND FINTROL

Biologists' weapons

Whereas poachers use a variety of illegal poisons to knock out fish, fishery biologists have their own sanctioned arsenal of about thirty chemicals that kill fish, also known as piscicides. Only two are commonly used in the United States: antimycin (Fintrol) and rotenone. Fintrol is an antibiotic that inhibits the fish's respiration. Rotenone is an extract from certain legumes that can be applied as a powder or liquid. It acts by blocking oxygen uptake, suffocating its victims. Both must be applied in doses that take into account such vagaries as the species targeted, the sizes of the fish, and water temperature. Fintrol is also highly sensitive to pH, with a half-life of five to eight days in soft, acid waters but only a few hours at pHs of 8.5 and above. Rotenone may be active for more than an hour after its application. Both rotenone and Fintrol can be detoxified with potassium permanganate. Different fish may respond at different rates: Some midwater species come to the surface almost immediately, whereas more sedentary fish come up much later. There is a tendency to become impatient when rotenone seems not to be working, and more rotenone may be applied, only to end up with an undesirable overkill of fish. Interestingly, rotenone treatments are nontoxic to most birds and mammals, but swine may be adversely affected.

Government agencies may use poisons to try to annihilate fish populations for at least two reasons. One is to estimate productivity of fish in a lake. By poisoning an arm or cove of a lake and then extrapolating to the entire water body, estimates of fish abundance and biomass may be obtained. The primary problem in such instances is restricting the poison to that portion of the lake; creating a wall of potassium permanganate is one solution. The other main reason for a legal chemical attack is when an unwanted fish species has been introduced into a water body. In smaller lakes, it is most efficient to simply kill all the fish present, then restock it with only the desirable species.

Rotenone received major publicity in 2002 as the weapon of choice in the battle against the snakehead. Small snakeheads are popular aquarium fish in the United States, with seventeen thousand of them imported between 1997 and 2000. But in their native range in China, these highly carnivorous fish reach three feet in length. When a hobbyist's pet snakeheads grew too large for their fish tank, he foolishly released the two fourteen-inch fish in a four-acre pond behind a strip mall in Crofton, Maryland. They were a male and a female, and they soon mated, filling the pond with their young. Because of the rapaciousness of snakeheads, officials feared that the fish might escape the pond and spread throughout the Chesapeake Bay drainage, eating and competing with native species wherever they took hold. Dispersal was likely, because snakeheads are remarkably hardy and may survive for days on wet ground, slithering to other water bodies.

In 2002, the pond was treated with rotenone, and Maryland's fish biologists held their breath. They were forced to exhale in 2004, when two snakeheads were caught by anglers in Maryland's Potomac River, a big system in which poisoning is impractical. Snakeheads may be in the United States to stay, and their impact remains to be seen.

Although rotenone is the poison of choice for biologists, it is a natural insecticide contained in a variety of plants, among them the South American genus *Derris*. In *Tales of a Shaman's Apprentice* (1994), ethnobotanist Mark Plotkin tells of a rotenone-based fishing expedition in the Amazon that he experienced the old-fashioned way. On the morning of the first day, he and about thirty Tirió Indians marched off into the forest to an area of large liana, or *ay-ah-e-yah*, vines. Machetes flashing, in twenty minutes they had a waist-high pile of foot-long segments that they bound on the spot with large leaves and bark strips into seventy-pound bundles. They hauled them back to the village, where they unloaded the wood at the edge of the river. They took turns crushing it with clubs and loaded the yellow pulp into dugout canoes. Then they went to sleep, exhausted.

Their journey the next day to the fishing spot began before dawn and ended near sunset on a beach. At daybreak the next morning, the women waded into the water and kneaded handfuls of the crushed *ay-ah-e-yah* pulp, releasing a whitish, bubbly substance that drifted with the current. Soon the men gleefully grabbed their bows and arrows and jumped into the canoes, one man paddling in the stern, the other standing at the ready in the bow. As the rotenone began to take effect, closing the capillaries responsible for taking oxygen from the water, the river surface started to boil with gasping fish—everything from baby catfish to piranhalike *pacu.*

The Tirió Indians are phenomenal marksmen and soon were impaling fish with one or more arrows, without a miss. And because the arrows were hollow but sealed, any fish that attempted to dive back down were floated back up by the buoyancy of the arrows. Plotkin likened the scene to a tropical ballet. Finally tempted to try shooting a large unconscious *pacu* himself, he found that the difficult feats of standing upright in a canoe, aiming at a fish underwater, and drawing a bow were impossible for him in combination.

In frustration, he attempted to reach for the *pacu* by hand. Just as he grabbed for the catch, an arrow passed between his third and fourth fingers, the Indian who shot it saying, "Better to not use your hands."

S

SALMON WEIR TRICKS

Using the fish's migratory instinct to the fisherman's advantage

The Pacific Northwest coast was home to untold numbers of salmon moving up streams and rivers to spawn. Because of the regularity and size of these runs, large Indian populations came to depend on them and invented many clever means of harvest. Some were straightforward, such as blocking the migrating fish with fence weirs or dip-netting or spearing them from wooden tripod stands. Another simple method involved building a collapsing fence at the narrowing of a tidal creek. The fence was left flat on the bottom on the incoming tide, and salmon swam over it, but when it was raised on the outgoing, the fish were trapped as the water level dropped.

More ingenious was to build two fences close together and parallel across a stream, but with the upstream barrier considerably higher than the other. Salmon could easily jump over the downstream fence, but they had too little room in the intervening space to gain sufficient velocity to leap over the second one, leaving them available for netting or spearing.

Another stream trap involved constructing a boulder dam with a wooden enclosure upstream of it. Salmon instinctively leaped the dam and found themselves corralled. To make spearing the fish

Native Americans netting salmon in front of opening in wooden weir across Trinity River, California.

easier in the roily water, white clamshells were used to line the bottom, heightening visibility. A variation was to build a log dam with an overhang on top and a boulder-lined pocket below. Salmon tried to leap over the dam but were blocked by the overhang, thereby accumulating in the pool and especially the pocket below.

A more elaborate trap used in swiftly flowing water involved a fence arced upstream in a pronounced U-shape, a much smaller concentric fence downstream with an opening at its apex, and a floor lined with slats that angled upward in the downstream direction. Salmon passed through the slot, encountered the upstream barrier, and then attempted to go downstream to locate a different passage. But as they moved back down, they'd slide up the sloping floor, from which they could be plucked.

It's also possible to shoot salmon with a rifle or shotgun before they leap. Salmon mass before obstacles as they attempt to pass them. When fish are apparent near the surface, a bullet or shot near the fish may be enough to cause temporary stupefaction, and the stunned fish can be retrieved by scoop nets or dogs.

SCENT ATTRACTANTS

Underwater perfumes

Fish can detect odors, and some, such as carp and catfish, have superb "noses." To make their baits and lures more attractive, some anglers apply folksy scents of questionable value, such as the lubricant WD-40, which has something of a cult following. But commercial compounds purposely made for fishing now come in many aromas, some based on serious research. A typical investigative approach is to soak cotton wads with one of several candidate scents, then plop these alternatives into a tank of hungry bass and watch their reactions. Garlic-scented crayfish reputably works well, but an angler could try attractants that invoke anise, sardine butter, hot sauce, shrimp oil, and banana oil. Some products even try that old "secret formula" approach. The makers of Crave Gravy claim it draws catfish because of its proprietary ingredient "SEXattract."

One theory behind the success of scent attractants is that they simply mask potentially off-putting odors that may end up on baits and lures, such as gasoline, oil, or tobacco. But because many of these scents are so pronounced, it seems that it must be more than that, and the fishing tackle industry is actively researching new possibilities. One company has performed roughly forty thousand experiments in trying to come up with a secret formula.

SHOOTING FISH WITH GUNS AND OTHER WEAPONS

A miss is better than a hit

Some large fish, such as giant halibut, are shot with guns at close range when being landed so that they don't hurt fishermen or destroy boats or gear. There is no pretense of sport in those instances, merely self-protection. But other fish unattached to fishing lines are plinked for recreation where they swim, and even when they fly.

Northern pike offer fine targets for shooting, because they often hold still in the shallows, waiting to ambush prey. The Vermont waters of Lake Champlain offer a short legal season for pike shooting. The weapon of choice is the .44 Mag Smith and Wesson Model 29 revolver, although any caliber of nine millimeters or larger should dispatch even the most ornery pike. They've also been shot with twelve-gauge shotguns using one-ounce deer slugs, and even deer rifles and AK-47s, but the use of these weapons may help define that grisly term "overkill."

Although one might assume that the body of the pike is the target, it's not so; the bullet should hit just below the fish, near its head. If the pike are hit, "you can't really eat them," says one fish hunter. "They just kind of shatter." The theory is that a close shot concusses and breaks the fish's air bladder.

My friend Rob Maass explored this fishery one April, not long after ice-out, when pike were moving into the backwater bays of the big lake to spawn. Sportsmen with guns were spaced here and there at the edge of a bay. Every once in a while a shot rang out, and the shooter then waded out to retrieve his pike. Some shooters climb trees or build platforms or "fish blinds" in them, as height is an advantage. So is experience; Rob often could not see the subtle waves made by the active pike, but his companion could, and a 30-30 bullet placed just under the fish resulted in pike doing loop de loops belly-up. Because large females may be attended by numerous smaller males, a lucky shot may produce, as one practitioner put it, "a big mare and six or seven little bucks."

Fish shooting is potentially dangerous, because bullets may ricochet off the water surface. It's better to aim downward than at an acute angle. Because of safety issues, it has been banned everywhere else in the United States, with the exception of Virginia, where for six weeks in the Clinch River, gun wielders may target bottom feeders such as quillback and redhorse suckers.

But not all fish shooting is performed legally. Angling writer Paul Schullery wrote about encountering a fellow with a .44 Magnum on the banks of a Montana river who was "shocking suckers." He'd shoot right next to one, stunning it, and then watch it drift away and revive—what might be called "blast-and-release fishing." Schullery, a refined fly fisher, resisted condescension, recalling his boyhood days plinking swimming minnows with a BB gun, the challenge coming from their diminutive size and the need to both lead them and correct for parallax.

One fish that offers sport more like traditional hunting is the mudskipper, a small, dark fish with turreted eyes. Mudskippers climb out of the water onto wet mud and mangrove roots, where they can be stunned by shooting them with rubber bands and then collected. Maybe those big eyes exist to avoid predators; hunters also have taken them with air rifles, rifles with "dust-shot" cartridges, small-bore shotguns, and slingshots.

Perhaps the ultimate in gunning fish is taking flying fish while in the air, performed at sea with shotguns much as in skeet shooting. Fortunately, these weird and tasty fish float when killed.

SKISHING

Dangerous but enervating

In *On the Run* (2003), David DiBenedetto includes a chapter titled, "Swimming with the Fishes." He means this literally, not as the old Mafia term for getting rid of a body in the drink. DiBenedetto is writing about skishing, the name for the very apex of the recently invented sport of extreme surf casting. Skishing was developed by Paul Melnyk to better reach large stripers in the rocky surf of Montauk, New York. It's not for the fainthearted, and Melnyk's approach has been described as on "the extreme end of extreme."

The concept behind skishing is that a wet suit–clad surf caster temporarily becomes a "vertical" boat as he bobs along with the current. DiBenedetto writes about a night-skishing foray with Melnyk himself. For obvious reasons, equipment must be minimal—essential items only. Before entering the water, the two skishers went through a checklist, which included flippers, a rod and reel, a few items of terminal tackle, and bait, as well as a headlamp, whistle, pliers, and knife.

Holding the bait while floating in the rollers is a problem, particularly because the favored offering is a live eel. The skisher's elegant solution is to keep them in individual Ziploc bags. The normally impossible-to-hold eel can be hooked through the bag and the plastic then torn away. On this night, Melnyk immediately hooked a striper, which, despite being the goal of the sport, presents problems in that with a long surf rod and a positively buoyant human, the fish has all the leverage. Thus the angler must lean back and kick to stay upright. Indeed, DiBenedetto's very first hookup while skishing plunged him facefirst into the water.

The inspiration for skishing was accidental. Since the 1960s, a few of the more adventurous Montauk surf-casting "rockhoppers" had been wearing wet suits to be able to swim safely to submerged boulders beyond wading distance. One day, while Melnyk was standing on a rock two hundred yards offshore and fighting a thirty-two-pound striper, a wave washed him off. The bass began towing Melnyk to sea, and with no chance of getting back onto the rock, he decided to fight the fish in its element. He found that if he placed the rod between his legs and floated on his back "like an otter eating an abalone," he could put some leverage on the fish. Five minutes later, he landed his prize, and a new sport was born.

But it was not one without clear dangers. Just moving out past the breakers wearing fins and holding gear is difficult enough, especially in rocky terrain. And because a skisher fishes well beyond the norm of land-based anglers, being run over by a motorboat is always possible, hence the whistle and, for daytime fishing, a bright orange or white hat. Then there are the currents. One copycat was swept toward the open ocean by a tidal rip. Fortunately, he had the presence of mind to drop his lure to the bottom, where it snagged and kept him in place until a boater noticed him.

Skishing can be seductive for the adventurous and physically fit surf caster. I had introduced a British friend, Mike Oliver, to Montauk surf casting, and he became so entranced that his autumn trips became the high point of his year. Eventually he wangled an invitation to skish with Melnyk. After his first try, in which he came back frozen and exhausted, he reported that he had never felt so alive.

SLATING

Caught between a rock and a soft place

This remarkably simple approach is practiced in the United Kingdom. The fisherman drills a hole near the middle of a piece of slate, passes a shot of cord through the hole, and stop-knots it. He then ties to the cord a length of fishing line with a hook attached, and buries the slate a few inches deep at the low-water line on a sandy beach. He dresses the hook with a robust bait, such as sand eel, to withstand surf action, and lightly covers it with sand to camouflage it from gulls.

Twelve hours later, after a full tidal cycle, the fisherman visits the slates, removing any fish caught and rebaiting the hooks. Slaters may fish up to fifty slates this way. The suction of the wet sand makes slates almost impossible to pull out, even by a large fish. But tope, a kind of shark, may rip smaller fish off the hooks.

SNAGGING OR SNATCHING

Subtle it's not

Although the fish hook usually is meant for the fish's mouth, it can readily pierce or snag the rest of the fish's body. Snagging, also known as snatching, can be awfully effective, though it is often scorned as crude and unsporting. But value judgments should be made in the context of circumstances. Snagging may be beneath or above contempt, usually depending on whether the species sought could be caught by traditional angling. For instance, along much of the Atlantic coast, menhaden are the supreme bait for stripers. The fish is kind of a chocolate bar for game fish, being composed of about 20 percent fat—many times that of other baitfish. But menhaden are filter feeders and steadfastly ignore bait or lures. So to acquire menhaden for bait, anglers must cast weighted treble hooks into surfacing schools and jerk them on the retrieve to impale them. Venture onto Long Island Sound in May and June when large stripers are migrating through and haunting the menhaden schools, and you will see boats everywhere with fishermen wildly yanking their lines through the water, looking as if they're trying to keep their offerings *away* from the fish. Not so—they're snaggers at work, and no one seems to begrudge them.

But snagging has a sorry history on the Great Lakes. These massive water bodies experienced major ecological perturbations that wrecked their native fisheries for lake trout and other game fish. Among the changes was the booming of alewives, a herring that overpopulated and then died off in huge numbers, subsequently rotting in harbors and on beaches. To provide a new game fish and help control the alewives, state agencies stocked Pacific coho salmon into the Great Lakes in the late 1960s.

The experiment was wildly successful; less than two years later, eight- to fifteen-pound salmon on their spawning runs filled tributary rivers. But both the agencies and the anglers were unprepared: The agencies did not have appropriate fisheries regulations in place, and the inexperienced anglers believed that the spawning salmon would not strike. Thus the fishermen turned to snagging. The banks were soon lined with fishermen lobbing weighted treble hooks into the flow to snatch salmon and fill their stringers. The newspapers called it "coho fever," but it was more an affliction than a celebration, as a crude "meat hog" mentality developed, with some fisherman filling their limits several times per day. Casters crowded the best pools, lines crossed, and ugly arguments and fistfights ensued. Snagging quickly became the standard tactic, and it was difficult for the agencies to wean fevered fishermen from it, but today most anglers entice salmon to the hook, and the riverbanks are more peaceful.

But although snagging has been outlawed in most places for salmon in the Great Lakes, a few clever anglers devised an unusual method that doesn't look like snagging, even though it is. Chinook salmon were stocked after the coho, and chinooks stage at the mouth of a particular river in Lake Michigan. The first pool is small, and the salmon tend to move around in circles. Fishermen in boats simply cast a spoon lure out and let it settle to the bottom. Sooner or later a salmon gets the line caught in its open mouth, and as it swims, it pulls the spoon off the bottom and into its jaws, resulting in a "strike."

Snagging has been put to better use in North Dakota, where it is used as a kind of fund-raiser. Paddlefish, great primitive relatives of sturgeon, dwell in large rivers and reservoirs of that state and much of the Midwest. But as plankton feeders, they don't strike bait or lures. North Dakotans have long snagged paddlefish, normally keeping the meat but throwing away the eggs, which can be made into a fine caviar. In an innovative program, the state allows anglers to snatch a limited quota of paddlefish for their own use, but the fish are cleaned by a nonprofit organization that keeps the eggs, prepares caviar from them, and then sells it on the international caviar market, using the proceeds to support environmental projects.

A rather direct form of snagging is practiced in the Indian subcontinent. When a massive catfish such as the gounch is located in a river pool, fishermen take turns swimming down to it and placing barbed hooks into its body. Each comes out with a rope leading to the hook. When three to five hooks are embedded, the fish is hauled out. Nepalese fishermen use pilks and jigs for "rip" fishing, in which fish are pierced anywhere in their bodies. These shiny lures, bearing anywhere from one to four sharp hooks each, are cast and then jerked up and down, using short rods; mahseer and snow trout are often taken this way.

As coarse as some forms of snagging are, the Japanese take it to the other extreme. The angler dresses in fine ceremonial costume and positions himself at low tide on a mudflat. Using a weighted treble hook on a line at the end of a long pole, he waits for the subtle raising of a mudskipper's head above the muck. Then, with phenomenal dexterity, he swings the hook and snatches the mudskipper in one movement.

SNARING

A poacher's trick

Looping a fine wire and drawing it tight around a live fish is an advanced art. One novice spotted a sucker under an overhanging bank in a stream. He stalked the fish, gently glided the snare into the water, and then slowly slipped the noose over the sucker's head. When he felt the moment was right, he jerked back mightily, but found the snare snagged in the boughs of a tree overhead. Where was the fish? Here and there—it had been cut in two.

Not all fish can be caught in snares. A long, thin body form is best suited to becoming stuck in a loop with a slip knot. In Russia's Ural River, stellate sturgeon were caught in snares made of one-millimeter-thick monofilament line. Eight- to ten-inch loops were set in a line across the current and held in place by weights. Sturgeon are bottom-grubbing fish, and as they root around for food, their long snouts easily poke through snares and other man-made objects. In

An approach to snaring gobies used by mountain peoples of the Philippines.

New York's famously polluted Hudson River, where human detritus is legion, many of us have seen sturgeon with rubber bands or the rolled ends of torn condoms wrapped around their snouts or heads, sometimes even girdling their growth. Sturgeon poachers like the snare approach because an attention-getting boat is not necessary—the rig can be tossed from shore.

In some ways, pike, with their long, slender bodies and tendency to remain motionless in the shallows as they wait to ambush prey, are perfect fish for snaring. They become even more so during spawning season, when they aggregate in marshes and are preoccupied with each other. In the 1800s, a British gamekeeper provided a detailed account of how poachers snare pike. This included selection of a long ash stick, slender enough to lie light in the hand but strong enough to bear sudden weight. A loop and running noose are formed from thin copper wire affixed to the narrow end of the stick. Loop size in relation to fish girth is important: too large and it will not draw up fast enough; too small and it may disturb the fish before it can be drawn.

Stealth is critical. In flowing water, the fisherman slowly lowers the noose to the bottom and allows it to drift with the current toward the pike, as if it were an ordinary twig or root carried downstream. The gamekeeper writes, "By degrees the loop comes closer to the fish, till with a steady hand the poacher slips it over the head, past the long vicious jaws and gills, past the first fins, and pauses when it has reached a place corresponding to about one-third the length of the fish, reckoning from the head." This location is said to provide a good balance of weight and straight "lines" of the body. The poacher then gets a good balance and, with a quick jerk, lifts the fish out and lands him on the "sward."

He adds, "The suddenness and violence of the compression seem to disperse the muscular forces, and the fish appears dead for a moment." Very often, in fact, it is; this usually happens when the loop is too close to the gills and garrottes the fish. Alternatively, a loop too near the tail often results in escape, with the pike falling back into the water but bearing a broad white band where the wire has scraped the scales. Fish marked this way were commonly seen in the water. Likewise, the way snared fish reached the market was often apparent to others from the loop's mark on its midsection.

Because pike gather when spawning, a skilled poacher could land a good basket of them. And because pike often lie side by side, and even in trios, it was not unusual to snare two at once. The gamekeeper once even saw a poacher safely land three at a time in the grass.

Snaring is especially useful in catching garden eels, a species that lives in sandy burrows with the head and forward portion extended to snap up plankton drifting by. When divers approach, the eels retreat into the bottom. But this opens up the possibility of a clever trick. While the eel is hiding, the diver places around the burrow a noose at the end of a long line, and then swims away a good distance. When the eel begins to reemerge, the diver yanks and the eel is lassoed.

Sri Lankans spend hours fishing the surf but avoiding the waves while sitting on makeshift stilt platforms.

STILT FISHING

Perched over the breakers

Among the exotic sights of Sri Lanka are fishermen reposing halfway up on giant poles sunk into the coral bottom. From these, they wield rods and take many fish from the surf below. Although this traditional approach is still used in Sri Lanka to take fish commercially, tourists may join the native practitioners for a fee. One who did reports, "It was a fantastic sight, about fifty of us clinging to the poles, while the waves broke all around us." Discomfort is the main drawback. The tourist was fortunate to be given a stilt with a bamboo basket to sit in, and still he was in agony by the end of the session, but many regulars sit only on thin poles. Despite its awful ergonomics, stilt fishing allows many fish to be caught in areas that are too rough and shallow for a boat, and too snaggy and distant to cast to from shore.

STONE SHELTER FISHING

Piscine foreclosures

Himalayan streams are unusual in that they receive tropical monsoon rains that cause them to swell greatly, yet their headwaters run from altitudes so high as to form glaciers. As soon as the postmonsoon floodwaters recede with the coming of winter, fish that ran upstream into enlarged brooks and creeks drop back to main-stem streams. But to escape the deep chill of these slopes, many small fish take shelter in rock crevices.

Locals capitalize on this by building stone shelters, little cold-weather Shangri-las. The fisherman usually chooses a shallow section near a deep-water pool and digs a circular depression of about two feet in depth and five feet in width into the rocky bottom. All around the shelter, he lays dead leaves and mossy stones to provide a natural setting. Then he places a long, flat stone over the top as a roof. Over the next few weeks, he adds more stones to attract more fish.

After about a month, the fisherman plugs the exit holes and encircles the shelter with a fine-meshed net, and then plucks all the surprised fish by hand.

STUNNING FISH THROUGH THE ICE

Smashing successes

Considering the harsh environments they're practiced in, some forms of ice fishing, such as jigging for bluegills, are surprisingly subtle. But not all. For a while after freezing and before the first snow, the ice on lakes is clear, and fish may be seen through it. In Russia, pike and burbot on occasion may be sighted in shallow lairs just under the ice. If a fisherman spots a fish, he may carefully approach and then strike the ice above it with a club or the flat side of an ax. If he makes a hole quickly, he can grab the stunned fish before it recovers.

This also has been done in Ireland, where it may become a social occasion. The loughs in County Cavan freeze solid enough to support groups of fishermen who, sometimes with the help of a dog, chase pike through the shallows until the fish tire, at which time the men smash a hole through the ice and haul the fish out with a hayfork. Fortunately for the pike of Ireland, the lakes of the isle do not freeze over every year.

The effect of the blow on the fish is called mechanical narcosis, the stupefaction resulting from vibrations. This effect also was known to the ancient Chinese, who knocked on stones with a hammer to stupefy fish that might be hiding beneath them.

SUCKER DRIVES

Startling sleeping fish

Driving suckers is an old technique used in the Catskill Mountains that appears to have slowly died out during the twentieth century. Suckers are bottom feeders common in the rivers and trout streams of these New York highlands. During winter, they aggregate in deeper pools. Although they are not highly regarded as a food fish when taken from warm water, in the cold months their meat is firm and tasty.

Two local news clippings tell of the methods and scale of sucker drives. A 1900 article describes one such drive: "The farmers for miles along the river get together and have what is called a fishing frolic. A long hole is cut in the ice about two feet wide and half-way across the river. In order to start the slothful, but toothsome sucker from his hibernating bed in the mud they employ a novel method. A great deal of noise must be made to start the fish and to do this they use their horses attached to mowing machines and hay rakes or with chains dragging behind. Even the children find amusement and are useful, for they follow behind with barrel staves with which they beat upon the ice to increase the racket."

This commotion drove the suckers toward the hole, where a dozen or more fishermen lay on their stomachs, ready with gaffs made from three hooks tied back-to-back and hung off a four-foot line attached to a broomstick-length hickory stick. When a fisherman sighted a large sucker, he slipped the hook beneath it, and with a quick jerk, the fish was on the ice.

Another article, this one from 1938, told of how a crowd of fishermen went after suckers and caught over one thousand of these fish, which were then often called "Delaware River Pork." It went on to state: "If anyone thinks there is no excitement in hooking suckers through the ice, he is wrong. It sounds like a pot arrangement but it is far from that. The hooker cuts a hole in the ice and bends over the hole with a long-handled hook while his companions go up or downstream and pound the ice to drive the fish his way. Then they begin to come in singles or pairs, then in bunches, the hooker begins to get excited. He hooks and misses till his arm is tired and the ice is covered with frantic struggling fish. They soon freeze stiff on a cold day, but thawed out once brought into the warmth they make excellent food." That weekend, a party took three hundred to four hundred pounds.

Catskill sucker drives continued until at least the 1970s, but more for tradition's sake than for necessary food. Over time, graceful gigs fashioned for this purpose from slim wooden poles and bent flexible steel replaced early, primitive gear; these reminders of this colorful fishery are still sometimes seen in local antiques shops.

SULAWESI SPIDERWEB FISHING

Silk lures sans hooks

Sulawesi spiderweb fishing is as odd as it sounds, yet that's what it is—the hookless "lure" is fashioned from actual spiderwebs. Fishermen on this Indonesian island seeking needlefish gather spiderwebs in the rain forest and then roll as many as ten to fifteen of them in their hands to form a sticky rope. While there in the forest, they also take a dead and dry palm leaf, tie a short length of the web "rope" to the end of a line, and then tie in the palm leaf yards above it. When the line is fed out and trolled behind their paddle craft, the wind lifts the leaf as a kite, allowing the lure to wiggle and bounce enticingly over the waves. Surface-feeding predatory needlefish soon take notice, attack the lure, and get their savage-looking teeth embedded in the sticky silk matrix. Sometimes a barracuda or mackerel also finds the lure irresistible. If the fisherman doesn't see the actual strike, he will soon notice the leaf being pulled down as the fish struggles.

This unique fishing technique is also highly sustainable. Not only is the spider allowed to go on spinning, but the silk lure can be reconfigured over and over again in the fisherman's fingers for up to three days' usage. But spiderweb lures become too slippery if they absorb oil, so fishermen must wash their hands well to prevent skin oils from cutting down on their catches. Wise fishermen also avoid coconut oil and hair pomade for at least three days before handling spiderwebs.

Similar forms of fishing are practiced elsewhere in the tropical western Pacific. In Tobi and other South West Islands, fishermen make the kite from a breadfruit leaf, drying it over a fire and pressing it flat under a sleeping mat. Then they thread the dried slender midribs of coconut leaflets through the breadfruit leaf, and tie them to one another where they cross to brace the leaf. They may fly these kites as high as three hundred feet while fishing. When working this rig from the reef edge, a fisherman may trim the leaf to direct it to a particular fishy location.

On Sonsorol, an island near Tobi, the species of spider that builds the appropriate web does not occur, and attempts by Sonsorolese fishermen to introduce it have failed. So Sonsorolese fishermen instead use the connective tissue that lies beneath the skin of lemon sharks. But this substitute is second-rate, because it becomes dry and leathery and must be chewed to make it supple again before each use.

In *Fishing from the Earliest Times* (1921), William Radcliffe cited A. E. Pratt, who wrote the provocatively titled *Two Years among the New Guinea Cannibals,* concerning an additional use of spiderweb for fishing. In New Guinea, the webs spun by spiders in the forests are six feet in diameter, with meshes that range from one inch near the outside to about one-eighth inch near the center. Native fishermen bent bamboo to form loops and placed them in promising locations. In a short time, a spider would construct a web, which the fisherman could use as a net that "resists water as readily as a duck's back, and holds fish up to a pound satisfactorily."

SURVIVAL FISHING

Whatever it takes

Although the Ancient Mariner may have had "water, water everywhere but not a drop to drink," other mariners have been stranded at sea or on islands with fish everywhere but no means to catch them. Survival fishing is not fancy and it is not sporting—it's whatever it takes to get the squirming bundle of protein in hand to keep starvation at bay. In most critical situations, obtaining food ranks low on the priorities list. Survivors often must focus on medical treatment, finding water and shelter, and contacting rescuers. But in many instances, people have been stranded at sea or on islands where catching fish was essential to remaining alive.

Life rafts should be outfitted with fishing survival kits. Sometimes the ones provided are comically insufficient, with flimsy hooks and a little string; such kits do nothing but save the vendor money and provide a false sense of security. A truly useful package should include a few basic lures such as jigs, an assortment of rugged hooks, various weights, and heavy-duty line.

Finding fish from a floating life raft in an infinite ocean might seem like a hopeless cause, but any survivors afloat have a major advantage in their favor: Many fish, particularly the widespread dolphinfish, are attracted to floating structures. One World War II sailor lasted eighty-three days adrift on a life raft after his ship was torpedoed by a German submarine off the coast of Brazil. After the stored food ran out at two weeks, he and his companions made a lasso from a twelve-foot rope and hung it over the side to try to snare sharks attracted to the hands and toes they hung over the side. They caught one on their second try and ate one meal before the meat went bad. Another day they captured eight small fish that wedged themselves into cracks in the raft as they attempted to escape predators. Seabirds also provided some awful but necessary meals.

On Thor Heyerdahl's famous journey across much of the Pacific on his raft, the *Kon-Tiki,* he found that flying fish were easily caught simply by setting out a little paraffin lamp at night. Flying fish were attracted by the glow and sailed, with some striking the sail or bamboo cabin and tumbling, helpless, on the deck. The adventurers often ate these fish for breakfast; one morning they gathered twenty-six. On another morning, the cook was upset because a flying fish struck him on the hand instead of landing right in the cooking fat.

Those attempting to survive on land can catch fish in rivers and lakes using traps made of sticks or wire. The basic design is a tube, with an internal conical opening that steers fish into the funnel opening. Placement of bait inside makes them far more effective. Survivors can fashion primitive hooks from a wide variety of materials, such as wire or thorns, or use slivers of wood to form a gorge. To avoid detection in hostile territory, a recommended set is the stakeout. The survivor drives saplings into the bottom of the body of water, with their tops just below the surface. He stretches a cord between them underwater, and ties short leads to baited hooks or gorges.

Spears can be made from a knife, jagged piece of bone, or sharpened metal attached to a sapling. It's better to jab the spear at a target than to throw it and risk losing the spear. A really primitive but effective survival fishing technique is chop fishing. If the survivor can use a light at night to concentrate fish nearby, he then can strike at them with a machete or similar weapon. But it's important to use the dull edge; the sharp side will cut them in hard-to-retrieve pieces.

Poisons are another weapon in the survivalist's arsenal. Although a fish researcher using chemicals to catch fish probably would never use these compounds, many plants and seeds are toxic to fish if used in strong enough concentrations. Of course, it helps if you are a botanist. Alternatively, lime works as a poison, cauterizing fish's gills. To obtain lime, the survivor can burn coral or seashells but needs to use it in small waters, as the recommended dosage is one ton per hectare.

Near the seashore, a tidal fish trap can supply easy catches. Below the high-tide line, the survivor can build a stone arc curving inland, and then deepen the hollow. As the next high tide recedes, small fish should be left behind.

SUSALERA MACHHA MARNE

Worms, melody, and rushing water

Susalera machha marne means, in Nepalese, "alluring bottom dwelling fish with whistling and splashing an earthworm garland over water." This specialized method is practiced in spring at the edges of crystal-clear pools and rapids of hill streams.

To do this, the fisherman must first gather earthworms, and then pin them to form a garland about four inches wide at the end of long, slender pieces of brush or bamboo. A cup-shaped collecting device also is necessary.

To draw fish, mainly loaches, the fisherman beats the garland rapidly at the water surface to generate both worm odor and vibrations while also whistling. (Westerners may be forgiven if they place more credence on the worm odor than the whistling.) When he sees fish biting the worm garland, the fisherman snatches it up and nets the fish.

SWIM FISHING, SURFBOARD FISHING, AND OTHER "SLEIGH RIDES"

Towing the line

Swimming-based fishing approaches keep being reinvented whenever an angler with a cowboy's daring tries to land large, sometimes dangerous prey while in the water, or just barely out of it, such as on a surfboard. A kid may try trolling in a lake while swimming on his back using the thrust of swim fins, but one experience with this gimmick is usually enough. (A British writer tells of a keeper's son who caught a large trout in forbidden water by swimming across it with a spinner tied to one of his legs; the method was described as chilly and tedious.) But in California, a cult of surfboard fishermen developed in the 1980s and included several hundred anglers up and down the coast.

The surfboard anglers drifted or paddled over kelp forests, those giant seaweed gardens that house myriad Pacific life. One of these anglers, Scot Cherry, was trolling for yellowtail with thirty-pound-test line when he hooked a thresher shark that was nearly as long as his thirteen-foot surfboard. The 140-pound fish towed Cherry almost six miles, at a speed fast enough to leave a wake. Cherry eventually gaffed the exhausted shark, pulled it close and ran his arm around it, then killed it by slicing his knife through its back.

That catch provided enough excitement for Cherry to make shark fishing his specialty. To increase his odds, he tows a bucket of chum and a bait bucket of live mackerel. He also keeps a knife and tourniquet handy. Once a large shark made a sudden dive and pulled Cherry eight feet under before he could begin free-spooling the line and swim back to the board. Over time, many of the California surfboard fishermen gravitated to kayaks, which may be a tamer approach but still allows the angler to be towed around by a big fish.

Sturgeon also have been known to tow people. When the Jim Woodruff Dam was built on Florida's Apalachicola River in the 1960s, it blocked the spawning run of the gulf sturgeon, fish that could reach hundreds of pounds. Soon boat anglers found that, baited with algae or worms, they could catch the goliaths that were stopped by the dam as they tried to move upriver. But to make it more sporting, fishermen began using inner tubes to ride the hooked sturgeon as they ran all over the river—hence the Apalachicola "sleigh ride." Unfortunately, even though sturgeon provide the world's best caviar, many fishermen didn't know what to do with their captures, and far too many sturgeon were left dead on the banks.

SWORDFISH HERDING

More challenging than sheep

The Bosporus is a narrow channel linking two huge inland seas: the Mediterranean and the Black. Water flows from the Black Sea, creating a strong current that ships have trouble navigating. The picturesque straits are lined with villas, whose owners at times have been awakened by prows of cargo ships crashing through their walls. So powerful is the flow around promontories that crabs have trouble swimming upstream. One such point is called the Cape of the Current, where the crustaceans are said to leave the water to cross the rocky spits by walking on land rather than bucking the current. This must have occurred for quite some time; the Greek writer Aelian declared in the second century that he himself saw that the crabs had gradually worn down a path.

Many sea creatures migrate seasonally between the Mediterranean and Black Seas. Among these are the once-abundant swordfish, large and delicious billfish that today are overfished and rarely seen anywhere inshore. A seventeenth-century historian of Istanbul, Evliya Celebi, describes how swordfish were caught at the village of Beykoz and other locations along the Bosporus: "There is a *dalyan* or structure for the capture of swordfish; it is composed of five or six masts, on the highest of which sits a man who keeps a lookout for the fish that come in from the Black Sea. When he sees them approaching, he throws a stone into the sea in order to frighten them, wherein he succeeds so well that they all head for the harbour, where they expect to find security, but instead swim into the nets laid in wait for them. The nets being closed, at a signal from the lookout, the fishermen flock round to kill them without their being able to make any resistance with their swords. The fish if boiled with garlic and vineyard herbs is excellent."

TICKLING TROUT OR HAND FISHING

"Groping for trouts in a peculiar river."
—**William Shakespeare, Measure for Measure**

The Bard was so tickled about tickling trout that he mentions it twice in his works. In *Twelfth Night; or, What You Will,* he writes, "Lie thou there; for here comes the trout that must be caught with tickling."

Tickling fish, usually trout (though even salmon may be tickled), seems an unlikely means of fishing. Not truly tickling, this hand-fishing technique might be described more as gentle grasping. There are many recommended variations. Some fishermen advise slowly mesmerizing the fish by stroking its belly. Another method, less artistic, perhaps, is to place one's hands below the trout and quickly flip it onto the bank. One writer even suggests fooling the trout by forming a false cave entrance with the hands. But it's not clear whether everyone who's written authoritatively on tickling trout has actually done so.

Why don't the fish simply flee in the presence of a palm and fingers? The theory is that because trout often hold in groups in prime lies during daylight hours, constantly brushing each other as they swim in the flow, a slow-moving, already chilled appendage does not feel radically different from the flank of another trout. The real problem is in getting a grip.

Michael Pewtherer, who spent a summer living off the land in New York's Hudson Valley, gives detailed instructions on tickling trout in the magazine *Wilderness Way* (2001, vol. 7, issue 2), based on his experiences with practicing this arcane art. To distill his advice: Move upstream to sneak closer to your upstream-facing quarry, and so that the sediment you dislodge doesn't cloud your fishing area. The vast majority of the time, you will not see the trout you are trying to catch, so your fingers must become your eyes underwater. Stay relaxed and move your hands, fingers limp, with the same characteristics as the water in which they are immersed. Let them flow with the current, exploring every possible hiding spot. Because trout are accustomed to brushing against other trout and having debris touch them as it tumbles past, the fish will not automatically bolt upon contact with a hand. So feel along its body to determine its size and to locate its head. For trout more than a foot long, cup both hands under the fish; keep one just before the tail, and use the thumb and middle finger of your other hand to find the gills. Then, being fast and severe, drive these two digits toward each other into the gills while gripping the tail with your other hand. You can take a smaller trout with one hand by placing your index and middle fingers around its head, and then clamping your other fingers as if making a fist. Be firm, but do both the one- and two-handed approaches gently enough to avoid harming the fish.

Hand fishing also is practiced in Nepal and many other places around the world. In fact, it's likely that hand fishing is mankind's original fish-catching method. However, its reputation has varied. A booklet published in Nuremberg in 1758 commented that it is a "fishery of the poor common folk who sometimes wish to bring home a small meal." British poachers took many trout this way, and even the slimy tench and large salmon. But hand fishing is popular and respected in Nepal, and individual fishermen there use a technique similar to that described above. They also may hand-fish in a file of about ten fishermen, who move their hands between stone crevices and flush fish, with fish that escape the hands of one fisherman often being taken by another. In a two-hour operation, ten hand fishermen may land as much as twenty-five pounds of fish.

Another accepted kind of hand fishing practiced by Northwest Coast Indians might be called hand steering. Diving, they grasped tired, spawned-out sturgeon by hand, and then guided them toward the bank as they swam.

Even something as simple and elemental as hand fishing is open to technological improvements. The Lengua Indians of Grand Chaco wrapped their hands with ribbons that have vertebrae fastened to them to afford a better grip on wriggling fish.

TIDAL WEIRS

Underwater fish corrals

In certain high-tide areas, cleverly designed weirs help fish trap themselves. Micronesians built stone weirs on reef flats to trap fish as the water receded. But nowhere does this work better than in the Bay of Fundy, home to the world's greatest tides, with changes as great as fifty-six feet. Sea level in the upper arms of the bay changes so fast that on a visit there on a falling tide, I noticed that each succeeding wavelet lapped lower on the shore. Fishermen long ago realized that by building long fences at strategic locations on the bay bottom, such extreme changes in water height would steer fish to holding areas, where they could be harvested at low tide. So effective are these weirs that they have taken as many as one hundred thousand shad on a single tide, in addition to the occasional shark, tuna, or porpoise. During the 1850s, the bay's Minas Basin had an average of one weir per mile; in the most favorable areas, there was a nearly unbroken line of weirs, their ends almost touching.

Today only a few are left. John McPhee describes a visit to one in his book on shad, *The Founding Fish* (2002). To recover the catch, he and the weir's operator rode down the rapidly emerging bay bottom on an all-terrain vehicle while towing a cart. Although the water fence was as much as seven feet high in its middle section, it soon was standing naked, three thousand feet long, on the bay floor. The weir was built almost parallel with the shore, but in a slight V-shape facing the sea.

The ingenuity of the trap, remarkably simple in design, lies in its interaction with shad behavior. At full high tide, as much as forty-five feet of water may cover it. As schools of shad follow the shoreline, trying to exit the emptying bay, they swim between the shallows and the long weir. By the time they reach the seaward end, the tide will have dropped enough to prevent them from turning its corner. But if they try to double back its more than half-mile length, its inland end also will have emerged from the sea. Then, as the tide drops further, all the fenced-off fish become conveniently trapped in a shallow pocket at the V-corner. Although the fishing is easy, the hours are not. By law, weir operators must tend the weir at every low tide, regardless of the time.

And there is another drawback: Building weirs is a laborious job, and they need to be constructed anew annually. Weirs are made with spruce and fir tree stakes, perhaps nine hundred for a single fence, cut and transported by the fisherman. In spring, he drags them out to the fishing site, but because the work must be done at low tide, the working window is only about two and a half hours—enough time to drive in only twenty-five or thirty stakes. Once all the stakes are in place, he weaves brush among them to form a wall. Eventually a primitive but highly effective weir stands ready to direct fish to their doom, but its life is short—the winter ice will tear it apart, and the fisherman will have to begin all over again the following spring.

TORCH FISHING FOR FLYING FISH AND NEEDLEFISH

Javelins in the darkness

Tobi Islanders of the South Pacific use torches to seek flying fish on black spring nights. Well after nightfall, fishermen paddle out to open water beyond the reef. This is done only on the twelve dark nights of the moon, because the palm frond torches are ineffective on bright nights when the moon drowns their light. Flying fish are famous for gliding above the sea surface for long distances—as far as one thousand feet—on their broad, winglike pectoral fins. But flying fish that are attracted to the domes of light usually approach underwater, where they can be readily dip-netted.

Another fish arrives airborne, however. Needlefish—long, thin fish that resemble piscine needles—may fly javelinlike past the fishermen. The fishermen, who traditionally go naked while torch-fishing, may be seriously hurt, or worse. At least two practitioners have died after being pierced by needlefish. When needlefish reach numbers deemed too hazardous, the chiefs call off torch fishing for the season.

Elsewhere, needlefish and similar species may be the targets of torch fishing. In Acapulco, Indians bearing harpoons go out at night in canoes for agujón, or "daggerfish," which may reach four feet in length. Here again, the fishermen choose moonless nights to maximize the attractiveness of light. These nights also allow for the greatest display of bioluminescence by plankton, this "fire in the water" enabling fishermen to see swimming fish by the light trails they leave. The harpooners light torches and watch closely, trident in hand. When the harpooner sees a fish setting for a leap toward the light, he can sometimes knock it down in the air and then spear it as it falls back. This form of fishing is beyond exciting; it's more like being a target in a shooting gallery, as several fish may leap from different directions at once. Daggerfish are aptly named, as many fishermen have died from wounds these fish have inflicted. One man was killed when he was stabbed through his throat; another was impaled through the eye. Daggerfish harpooners are easily recognizable by the ugly, puckered scars they bear.

TROLLING INNOVATIONS

It doesn't have to be a drag

Trolling—the technique of towing lures or baits behind a moving vessel—is one of the least popular but most productive forms of fishing. Many find it profoundly boring. But trolling covers a lot of water, and trollers may be more likely than still fishermen to intercept fish.

The major issue with trolling is that when you pull a lure and line behind a boat, the drag of the water makes the offering rise high, whereas the fish usually are in the lower depths. Part of trolling's lackluster reputation is because of the need to use stout tackle and heavy weights to compensate for drag and to fish deeply.

But trolling as a viable approach has probably existed as long as hook-and-line fishing itself. Northwest Indians trolled for salmon from canoes, keeping their lines tied around their paddles; each stroke gave life to the sprat bait. According to one observer, the moving paddle "keeps the fish in constant motion, so as to give it the appearance of life, which the salmon seeing, leaps at it and is instantly hooked, and by a sudden and dextrous motion of the paddle, drawn on board."

Until recently, techniques used to troll deeply relied either on weight or on angled devices that pulled downward as the line pulled forward. In the Finger Lakes, anglers trolling for lake trout used complicated rigs that included hefty weights on the ends of cable to which they had clipped lines with lures at intervals to fish at different heights off the bottom. This was definitely productive, but not at all sporting. Another weight-based approach was to use a metal line that cut through the water by its own weight. One hundred yards or more of stainless steel or Monel wire could carry a lure down far. These stiff strands overpowered most fish, however, and also often kinked and broke. Planer boards could sink an offering by providing a downward physical vector, but the force of resistance needed was strong and made holding the rod difficult; also, the planer was a hindrance in fighting any fish hooked.

Fortunately, an ingenious invention put the sport back in trolling: the downrigger. Downriggers are weight-based devices, but the key to their popularity is that the weight is not attached to the angler's line; in fact, the reverse is true—the angler's line is attached to the weight. The fisherman lowers the sinker, known as a "fish" because it usually is somewhat fish-shaped to cut through the water, to fishing depth off a cable that he operates manually or electrically from a device that includes a reel and short arm. Before lowering the sinker, the fisherman attaches his line and lure or bait to the cable with a special release clip, places the fishing rod in a rod holder, and tightens the line enough to put a strong bend in the rod. When a fish strikes the lowered bait or lure, the line releases from the cable, and the rod springs upward reflexively to set the hook. Rods for this purpose often are long to provide a lengthy sweep. If the angler successfully strikes the fish, he can enjoy the fight unencumbered by any weight.

Offshore fishermen also may employ outriggers. These are long, usually fiberglass poles that flare outward from the sides of the boat. Anglers seeking big game fish such as tuna or billfish like to present a variety of lures or baits in a wide pattern behind their vessels as they troll, and running lines to the ends of the outriggers greatly increases the width of the area covered. As with downriggers, when a fish strikes, the line disengages, and the angler can fight the fish directly. An alternative to outriggers is planing boards, which use water resistance to pull the line sideways away from the vessel. These "sleds" are towed off their own lines and are rigged with clips to release the fishing line. Santa Catalina Island Tuna Club members developed heavy-duty marine sleds for those times when it was too calm or too windy for their favored kite rigs. These sleds were three feet in length and connected sideways to one hundred feet or more of running line, at the appropriate angle to ride but not bury in the waves. The angler attached the fishing line somewhere in between and adjusted it so that the bait skipped along over the water surface.

Although they are primarily offshore tools, planer boards are sometimes used in fresh water to present lures close to shallow structure. This includes in Florida's man-made "box-cut" canals, which may be perfectly linear and lined by sheer vertical banks, which is where the game fish reside. A boat can ride right down the middle and fish lures alongside both walls at once.

A recently invented trolling trick used by offshore game fishermen in clear ocean waters is to adorn their boat hulls with baitfish images, using decals or stencils. A traveling vessel with an array of these representations may pass as a school of prey to a marlin or tuna. One stencil purveyor offers a choice of squid, mackerel, shiner, or flying fish.

Perhaps the most advanced practitioners of dragging lures behind boats are professional salmon trollers. The attractiveness of this approach is that the salmon are landed and then handled individually, so they remain in top condition and fetch the highest prices. But to land enough salmon to make it pay, these fishermen must drag many lines, and as anyone who has fished multiple rods in close proximity knows, it's awfully difficult to keep them untangled. Salmon trollers use almost every conceivable gambit to spread their offerings: outriggers to present lines laterally, float lines with float bags that suspend vertical lines held down by weights with lures at various levels, and deep lines that drop as much as eighty fathoms off the stern, also with spreads and weights.

Trolling is really the act of towing a bait or lure through the water, which usually involves a boat, but doesn't have to. Striper anglers fishing off a bridge at night may amble along the railing, letting their line dance along the magical "shadow line" that marks where the structures' lights meet darkness and where the game fish set up their ambush. And in Washington, D.C., fishermen "walk-troll" the seawall in East Potomac Park for largemouth bass.

TROTLINING

A Deep South tradition

Trotlining, like jugging, is a truly old-fashioned catfishing approach. A trotline is made up of a strong rope with a series of baited hooks attached. Anglers can suspend trotlines off floats or stretch them between shore and anchor, usually setting them near dusk and then checking them every hour or so. Potential baits are endless; some held in high regard are turkey livers, hardback shrimp, crickets, and soap that's been microwaved just long enough to soften it. One midwestern flathead catfish specialist liked to use live pound-and-a-half goldfish. He found that the first five hooks from the bank always took the largest cats, because these fish cruised near shore while seeking raccoons or skunks to eat.

An ostensibly trotlined catfish is at the center of a historical controversy. When Betty Coleman, from Savannah, Tennessee, was looking through old black and white photos at the Hardin County Historical Society, she stumbled across an image difficult to believe. In it, a man stands at the rear of a carriage on which is draped a giant flathead catfish several times his size. She later learned that the photo was taken in the Hardin County community of Cerro Gordo in 1914, and that the picture had hung for many years in a local general store. Supposedly a fellow named Green Bailey caught the fish on a trotline, and, in fact, his name and Cerro Gordo 1914 are engraved on the photo. If authentic, the fish is estimated at five hundred to eight hundred pounds.

But a recent investigation uncovered other stories: that it was caught by the owner of the general store, that it was caught by hand after it became landlocked in the shallows during a drought, and that it was a hoax. Many believe that the catfish actually weighed only fifty to eighty pounds and that it was placed on a child's wagon, with a cardboard cutout of a man from a cigarette ad. This theory gained credence when it was learned that a second photo exists, but from the front of the wagon, and that despite the different angle, the man is in exactly the same position: side view, one hand on his thigh and the other on his hip. In any event, the photo does nothing but help toward the promotion of the National Catfish Derby, held on the Tennessee River, and Hardin County, which bills itself as the "Catfish Capital of the World."

Sometimes anglers catch the wrong prey while trotlining, such as a nasty snapping turtle. Worse yet, one novice tried trotlining for a couple nights without success, then left the rig in his backyard, only to hook an angry opossum.

TROUT- AND SALMON-POACHING TECHNIQUES

A sneaky suite of tricks

In the old British system, fishing rights in rivers and streams were the property of landowners, who often rented them for high fees and hired gamekeepers to protect their interests. But poor villagers and other locals could watch the runs of delicious salmon and sea trout, not to mention the resident trout, and many were tempted to take some for their own use or for sale. A cat-and-mouse game developed between keepers and poachers. The latter became quite sophisticated, with stratagems such as fishing in groups, using a lookout, and employing diversionary tactics.

Crude poaching approaches included poisoning streams with chloride of lime and spearing salmon on their spawning redds. But poachers also used more subtle methods. To catch an old cannibal brown trout, poachers baited a stout line, tied it to a tree root, and left it overnight to tempt the night feeder. Another tactic was to use two stones to weight a long line with baited dropper lines; this setup was almost impossible to detect, but the poacher could retrieve it with a hooked stick or grappling hook. Or he could hang a line with a fly spoon to a wispy branch trailing in a fast stream. The trout would hook and play itself until exhausted, and the poacher could retrieve it at his leisure. When a stream was receding after a heavy rain, a poacher could set a dozen short lines for the trout he knew would be hunting for insects and worms that had washed in; a pipe smoke and twenty minutes later, a few fish would be on the lines.

Another poacher's gambit, one that required a little patience, was to hang the head of a sheep or other animal from a tree over a trout pool. Inevitably, flies infested it, and their young—wiggly maggots—began to fall into the stream, clustering trout at the site. Such fish were easy marks for a maggot drifted on a small hook.

A completely different form of salmon poaching was conducted by a higher British class. Two centuries ago, the lords of the manor at the Falls of Kilmorack on the River Beauly would set up a boiling kettle on a flat rock on the south side of the cascade. Guests relaxed in tents and watched as salmon attempted to vault the falls. Some fish did not make it and fell back. If the group was patient, eventually a salmon would land right in the kettle, where it would become, of course, poached.

U

UNCONVENTIONAL LONG-DISTANCE CASTING

Superhuman casts are not a casual endeavor

There have been many attempts to invent alternative means to the standard rod and reel to deliver an angler's offering a long distance, such as the surf bow and reel, a bow designed to shoot line and bait out over the waves. Very few of these novelties have caught on. But I once did see an approach that was stunningly complex but nonetheless successful. During a fisheries conference in Portland, Oregon, I was invited on a field tour of the lower Columbia River. We parked at an overlook just downstream of the giant Bonneville Dam, a concrete colossus that can generate as much as half a million kilowatts of electricity. My colleagues were awestruck by the scale of the barrier and the currents that roared from its orifices, but I was transfixed by a group of sturgeon fishermen who employed the most specialized casting gear I'd ever seen.

The anglers sat on lawn chairs and watched their rods, the lines from which appeared to stream to eternity. The incentive for making superhuman casts was that public access from the overlook was on one side of the river, but the trough that held the sturgeon was on the other side, two hundred yards away. The system that had evolved to reach the lie involved two separate rods plus a large flowerpot. One rod was the casting rod, long and powerful, but lacking line guides or a reel. The other rod was the fighting rod, and this one had guides and a reel.

The system is a complicated balance of trade-offs. For fighting large fish, a conventional reel, with its line feeding directly onto the spool, is a better choice than a spinning reel. But in routine use, spinning reels are more easily cast than conventional reels. With a spinning reel, the line simply peels off the spool without forcing the spool to turn, whereas the revolutions of the spool of a conventional reel generate cast-shortening friction. But for extreme distance casting, spinning fails, because friction with the lip of the spool increases rapidly as the line remaining on the spool dwindles.

Theoretically, then, a large spinning reel without a lip would be the best choice of all, but it wouldn't be practical for angling. An exception, though, is when a bait can be fished for hours after a cast. Indeed, these specialized sturgeon fishermen used a giant spinning reel; this was the large flowerpot on a homemade mount, its tapered bottom facing toward the river and oriented about forty-five degrees upward, like a cannon. Each cast required a considerable investment of time. First the angler placed the fighting rod in a rod holder. He pulled the right amount of line from the tip-top— enough line to reach the sturgeon holding area—and carefully wound it around the flowerpot. But he left the end of the line plus the terminal tackle free, which he then attached to the casting rod.

The terminal tackle was designed with long-distance casts in mind. In addition to a sinker, the angler used a short leader to the hook, because a long leader would whirl and generate air friction. The bait was small (a hunk of lamprey or shad) and was held down with elastic thread so it wouldn't fall apart on the cast or underwater. Some of these anglers sprayed their baits with WD-40, not because it might cut down on wind resistance, but because they believed it attracted sturgeon. The line to the sinker sometimes had a lesser breaking strength than the main line. The angler then attached the free end of the main line to the casting rod so that a length hung off a clip at its tip, the clip being attached to a thumb trigger.

Once he was thus rigged, the angler moved near the railing, arced the casting rod, and drove it forward while releasing the thumb trigger. The sinker then shot high out over the river, pulling line off the flowerpot freely and with virtually no friction. When it hit bottom, it immediately snagged among the rocks, holding the bait in place. The angler then adjusted the line to run straight to the fighting rod, and the wait began. Eventually a sturgeon might take the bait, and if hooked, the line to the sinker quickly broke. This remarkably elaborate endeavor was worth it: The quarry might measure eight to ten feet and weigh hundreds of pounds.

Such a reward has motivated other anglers to invent other means to reach far-off sturgeon. A retired school bus driver in Washington rigged a giant slingshot to the side of an ancient Volkswagen Beetle. By rearing back about twenty feet on the rubber sling, he could fire his railroad spike sinker and bait well out into the Columbia River. Another slingshooter, known as "Slingshot Bob," made his state-of-the-art device from a trailer hitch, two-and-a-half-inch square steel pipe, four pieces of eight-foot-long surgical tubing, and a homemade leather pouch. Earlier versions were not foolproof and sometimes were downright dangerous, shooting eight-ounce sinkers sideways and even backward. But Slingshot Bob perfected his approach; now he pulls way back, releases, and delivers his bait accurately to sturgeon swimming two football field lengths away.

Homemade slingshot used to shoot bait and terminal tackle for sturgeon far out into the Columbia River.

UNNATURAL BUT EDIBLE BAITS

Supermarket and slaughterhouse as bait shops

Wooden, plastic, and metal artificial lures are both unnatural and inedible. Another odd class of baits consists of those that are unnatural but edible. Fish will never encounter these in nature, yet they still work to seduce fish.

This broad category is dominated by baits for catfish. Many catfish attractants can be found at a neighborhood grocery store; in fact, fishing with these products has been called Krogering, after the food store chain. Standard frankfurters work well, as do fancier ones with cheese inside. Pros go further though, injecting them with liquid flavor enhancers such as cod liver oil, anise oil, or chicken blood. Catfish also like canned dog and cat foods, but these can be difficult to keep on the hook. To solve this problem anglers cut a piece of surgical tubing just long enough to fit over the hook shank, and then pack it with moist pet food. Catfish anglers also chum with pet food.

Catfish will eat soft cheese, as will trout. Garlic cheese, in particular, delivers a potent scent. From the seafood counter, old shrimp ready for the dumpster is a catfish treat, as is liver—beef, deer, chicken, rooster, or turkey—from the meat section. Rooster and turkey liver are popular because their toughness keeps them from falling off the hook better than the more easily obtained chicken liver. Liver has also been used at sewer outlets around Manhattan Island for striped bass.

A relatively new catfish killer is called "bloodbait." It has been made from the blood of goats, horses, lambs, deer, rabbits, geese, chickens, turkeys, and even emus. It seems that anything that bleeds and is warm-blooded is fair game. But bloodbaits are not all equally effective, and users have their favorites. One bloodbait maker, known as "Cat Daddy" Shumway, started with chicken blood but has come to favor turkey blood, because it's easier to acquire in large quantities, coagulates faster and thicker, and when fished, "bleeds" more and for a longer time. But both are more tender than beef blood, which stands up better while being drift-fished.

Making bloodbait is not for the queasy or fainthearted. At the slaughterhouse, Cat Daddy pours blood into fifty-gallon barrels and loads them onto a trailer. During the ride home, vibrations conveniently cause the congealed blood to sink to the bottom of the barrels. As soon as he arrives home, Cat Daddy pours off the liquid blood, saving it for his special chum mixture of wood chips, sour grain, and maggots. He then places the congealed gore in a plastic wading pool. From there, he can make unseasoned or seasoned batches, possible flavors including garlic, anise, or menhaden oil. After broadcasting the seasoning, he sprinkles sugar over the surface, which causes the ingredients to roll over and mix. After two days of brewing, the bubbles stop and the mixture is ready for freezing. Later, to toughen the clots, Cat Daddy defrosts the blood and leaves the liverlike slabs on concrete in the hot sun. He adds kosher salt, and then refreezes them.

Not all catfish anglers like to cope with the fragility and messiness of pure bloodbaits, but there are alternatives. Bob's Cheese Punch Bait, developed by a Texan, Bob Fincher, is a select mix of cheese, ground chicken guts, and blood—what is there for a catfish not to like? It's called Punch Bait because to rig up, you punch your treble hook down into it with a stick, then grasp the line and withdraw it, now holding a gob of Punch Bait. A recent competitor is Cat Candy, which includes cattail reeds, sour soybeans, turkey blood, anise, and flour. As the mixture ages, it becomes rank with maggots, but this is not a bad thing. Once the maggots have grown, the angler freezes the stew long enough to kill the grubs, then defrosts it and stirs it to better intermingle the maggots with the rest of the bait. It seems that the possibilities for the creative catfish bait maker are endless.

V

VINGLING FOR SAND EELS

Beware of weevers

Vingling is a little-known English technique in which the fisherman pulls a knifelike tool with a hook-shaped tip through wet sand above the tide line. What would a vingler find in such a strange fishing location? Sand eels, of course.

The best places to vingle are banks next to pools of standing water—always in wet, not dry, sand. The vingler draws the knife repeatedly toward the body in short strokes no more than four inches deep. The blade cuts through the sand easily until an eel is trapped, when there is a definite resistance. A good vingler feels the wriggle of the sand eels through the knife and pulls upward, catching the fish in the crook of the tool. He lifts the blade upward rapidly and grabs the sand eel the moment it emerges from the sand, before it falls off and burrows right back down. Real pros can draw the fish out and flick it into a bucket, which is faster in the long run. But a less-skilled vingler may lose many, because these fish disappear back into the sand at amazing speed.

Surprisingly, an activity as seemingly innocuous as vingling can be dangerous. The poisonous lesser weaver fish has the same burrowing habits as the sand eel. Grab one of these and its spines can leave the fisherman in excruciating pain and in need of medical care. Remarkably, experienced vinglers can feel the difference in re-sistance between the two species while either is still under the sand.

Other dangers may also befall the determined vingler as he is working, hunched, eyes on the ground. A local from St. Ives, Eng-land, was working a beach one night, looking for that first sand eel to begin fishing with. As he moved backward, he felt the resistance of a large sand eel, but before he could draw it up, it slipped the blade and escaped. Encouraged because where there's one, there's usually more, he continued to vingle. As he felt the next eel, he en-countered something against the back of his boot that caused him to stumble. He planted his other foot on top of a large, moving ob-ject that howled and snorted, frightening him off the beach. It turned out to be a seal, equally frightened.

WATERFALL FISHING

Because they leap before they look

A passive approach that must have been especially fun to watch as it fished was a waterfall trap. This tactic was not based on trickery; in the old days, there were so many salmon that sufficient numbers simply landed in the traps by chance.

Pacific salmon are famous for leaping waterfalls, but not every vault is successful. Indeed, the higher the falls, the fewer the fish that make it. Those that don't often descend through the air somewhat in front of the water plume. To catch falling salmon, Native Americans constructed an L-shaped grid below the falls, just far enough away to allow the fish room to leap. Should a salmon fail to scale the waterfall, voila! Gravity neatly placed it in the jaws of the trap, which was tilted slightly backward like a mouth.

Variations of this approach are found elsewhere around the world. Near Windau, in Latvia, fishermen hung baskets onto a waterfall that salmon leaped over, in order to catch fish that didn't successfully make the vault. And in both North America and northern Europe, fishermen built salmon boxes, sluiceways placed on waterfalls so that a distinct salmon-attracting plume spilled from them. These boxes had a baffle that a leaping salmon could clear, but that would then prevent the fish from falling back downstream, while another barrier kept them from moving upstream. The sluiceway also had a roof so that the fish could not leap the barriers.

In Nepal, snow trout (not a member of the true trout family) take fantastic leaps to ascend through mountain torrents to their upstream spawning grounds. Fishermen here make simple woven traps to catch leaping snow trout. A flat, rectangular woven panel about twelve to twenty feet long and three to five feet wide has a "fallback" pocket attached to its bottom. The fisherman hangs the whole framework over a suitable waterfall from branches arranged crosswise on the rocks. Placement is critical: The jet of the waterfall must pass through the gear. The angler sets the trap in the evening and collects its catch in the morning.

Snow trout of several species all leap by clearing the water while beating their tails against it to build speed, and then spreading their fan-shaped pectoral and ventral fins to glide almost like flying fish. Because they orient to the flow in trying to leap barriers, they fly right into the mesh wall, only to fall back into the basket.

Then there is the fanciful old trick of the desperate trout fisherman. Paint a waterfall on the side of a boat. Park it crosswise in the middle of a stream. Hope to see trout jump into the boat.

WEIRD HOOKS

Elaborate constructions that were painful to lose

To anyone buying the now widely available, chemically sharpened Japanese fishhooks, what passed for fishhooks in olden times may seem comical. But necessity begets invention, and these primitive fish catchers were very much state-of-the-art for their time—and perhaps even for today.

The design and craft of these early hooks sometimes were amazing, and it must have been painful to lose one. Klamath and Ojibwa Indians made complicated hooks with about six parts; hooks made by Pukapukans had a remarkable fifteen components. Some early Europeans, accustomed to metal forms, scorned the stone, bone, seashell, wood, or coconut shell fish-hooking devices of Pacific islanders and other native cultures. But other Europeans who actually tried them favored these devices over European designs. One admirer described them as "a triumph of stone age technology." Captain Cook said of Hawaiian hooks, "Considering the materials of which these hooks are made, their strength and neatness are really astonishing; and in fact we found them upon trial, much superior to our own." The design flaws of European hooks made from metal were so obvious to Tahitian fishermen that they sometimes reshaped them, often cutting off the barb. European conceit also deflated upon contact with natives of British Columbia and Alaska. One explorer writes in 1855 that the "apparently clumsy" hooks of the region possessed so many advantages over the type used by Europeans that they were still retained despite the availability of the European style.

Tobians have thirteen different categories of fishhooks. Some are generalized hooks that the angler uses until it's apparent which fish species are available, after which he switches to specialized styles. One unique design is called a *haufong,* which has a bent tip with no barb. It was designed for the hard-jawed but tiny-mouthed triggerfish. When the fish nibbles on the baited tip, it penetrates the roof of the fish's mouth, allowing the shank to slide through until the fish is well secured on the hook's V-shaped crotch.

Micronesians made hooks from the shells of hawksbill turtles (green turtle shells were too weak) and of various mollusks. They probably sharpened them using coral as sandpaper, finishing them off with the abrasive skin of rays. Although hooks are more effective for catching fish, anglers often used wooden gorges that wedged sideways in fish's mouths, because a good turtle-shell hook took two or three days to make, whereas a gorge could be fashioned in minutes. Some turtle-shell trolling hooks had not only a conventional barb, but also a barb on the main shaft opposite it. The fisherman used these while trolling two lines; if fish were on each line, he could hold one on the hook while retrieving the other. The making of shell hooks required such an investment of time that they were not easily forsaken. On Tobi, if a grouper ran into a hole in the reef with a hook, the angler did not break off the line and sacrifice the hook. Instead, he kept steady tension on the line until the grouper swam out, as much as an hour later.

Some cultures made hooks from composites. Indians in British Columbia constructed tiny fishhooks from wood tipped with slender bone barbs; northern Scandinavians used these materials together as well. Northwest Indians also made hooks with stone shanks carved to receive a bone barb at the correct angle for halibut, whose name, translated, meant "great one coming up against the current." An advantage was that the hook acted as its own sinker.

These Indians also used bentwood hooks—hooks formed into a strong U-shape—with a bone barb lashed to the tip with split spruce or cedar root. Making these hooks was no simple task. First the angler shaved fir driftwood branches to the right thickness and shape. He placed them into kelp tubes cut from the bottom of the plant so that the root capsule held water, plugged the ends of the tubes, and soaked the sticks overnight in the hot ashes of a fire. The next morning, when the sticks were pliable, he pushed them into a U-shaped mold. After cooling, he scorched them once, rubbed them with deer tallow, and placed them back in the mold to prevent the hook from opening out again.

Barbs also took some effort to make. The angler splintered or sectioned mammal bone and sanded down the resultant fragments. He then lashed these barbs onto the wooden hooks, and they were ready to be fished. Contrast that with today, when we can simply order our hooks via the Internet.

Unlike metal hooks, wooden hooks are buoyant, and this property was an integral part of the hooks' success. The wooden hook would float up from the weight that secured it, with the barb aimed down. If a halibut tried to seize the baited barb, the hook's large gap would stop the fish from ingesting it. Halibut, like many other fish, forcibly expel items they can't swallow. In doing this, they drove the barb into their cheek, thereby hooking themselves. When the fishermen began adapting iron barbs to wooden hooks, the hooks were no longer buoyant, so they added small wooden floats, often elaborately carved as fish or mammals, to position them properly.

Some anglers used wood taken from a knot in decayed hemlock to make a variation of the bentwood hook that they employed mainly for black cod. This hook relied on a spring action that would bring its arms together. The fisherman tied the bait in a tucked position behind the barb and used a wooden peg to keep the gap open. When the fish struck the bait, the peg dislodged and the arm closed, keeping the catch on the barb.

In *Pattern of Islands* (1952), Arthur Grimble wrote about how natives of the Gilbert and Ellice Islands grew their own hooks. Absent metals, they fashioned hooks from wood. To catch tiger sharks, sturdy ironwood worked best. To obtain the right shape, the fisherman bent a twig of an ironwood tree and lashed it into position so that it recurved on itself. The angler needed great patience: He cut the wood when it was about a half inch thick—which took years.

WHAT TO DO IF ALL ELSE FAILS

You can always resort to magic or whiskey

Sometimes nothing an angler tries yields the desired catch. When this happens, one option is to use magic. Among the Nootka Indians, a wizard would construct a swimming fish of wood and launch it in the direction from which the schools usually arrived. This simulacrum, together with the proper incantations, was believed to compel the laggards in no time. In Scotland, fishermen dogged by ill luck would throw one of their own overboard and then haul him out exactly as if he were a fish. This ruse apparently whetted the fish's appetite, for "soon after trout, or sillock, would begin to nibble."

Speaking to a group of fish scientists gathering information on alternative means of catching specimens, American Museum of Natural History curator Melanie Stiassny offered this advice gleaned from her time in Africa: "Sit on a river bank with a bottle of whisky and wait. After two minutes some young men will appear from nowhere. Tell them (either verbally if in ex-British or Francophone colony, or otherwise by gesture) that you will pay them a princely sum for each fish they bring you. Sit back, relax, drink whisky and wait."

Then again, sometimes it's okay to let the fish win and just leave them in the water.

ART CREDITS

1, 2, 63, 111, 100: Caroline Stover.

18, 37, 105, 154: *Guide to the Classification of Fishing Gear in the Philippines*, Agustin F. Umali, illustrations by Silas G. Duran, United States Government Printing Office, 1950.

21: *Old Fishing Lures and Tackle*, 6th edition, KP Books.

30: *A Naturalist in British Columbia*, vol. 1, John Lord, 1866.

32: Library of Congress, Prints & Photographs Division, FSA-OWI Collection, LC-USF34-070151-D DLC.

34: *Fishing from the Earliest Times*, William Radcliffe, 1921.

44: Janet Hayden.

47: *The New York State Conservationist*, December–January 1953–54.

60, 61: Warwick Kershaw.

73: NOAA National Marine Fisheries Service.

76, 77: John Waldman.

101: Danilo Cedrone, FAO, NOAA Central Library.

115: *Fish Catching in the Himalayan Waters of Nepal*, Tej Kumar Shrestha, 1995.

iii, 122, 123: Drawings by Andras Csikos-Toth and Roger Humbert. Reprinted from *Sturgeon Hooks of Eurasia* by Geza de Rohan-Csermak (Viking Fund Publications in Anthropology, #35, 1963) by permission of the Wenner-Gren Foundation for Anthropological Research, Inc., New York, New York.

138: *Pacific Fisherman*.

146: McCormick Library of Special Collections, Northwestern University Library.

156: Ludovic Galko Rundgren.